FAST MUSCLE BUILDING

15 Bodybuilding Secrets to Grow Drug-Free Lean Muscle Mass

Using Natural Supplement Stacks and Strength Training Workouts

FAST MUSCLE BUILDING

15 Bodybuilding Secrets to Grow Drug-Free Lean Muscle Mass

Using Natural Supplement Stacks
And Strength Training Workouts

By Coach Rob Regish
Foreword by Carl Lanore

STRATEGIC EDGE INNOVATIONS PUBLISHING
Los Angeles - Toronto

FAST MUSCLE BUILDING
15 Bodybuilding Secrets to Grow Drug-Free Lean Muscle Mass
Using Natural Supplement Stacks and Strength Training Workouts

1ˢᵗ Edition. 2016

Copyright © 2016 by Coach Rob Regish
and RSR Fitness Systems, LLC

CoachRobRegish.com

All rights reserved. No part of this book may be reproduced or transmitted in any form or by any means, electronic or mechanical, including photocopying, recording or by any information storage and retrieval system, without written permission from the author, except for the inclusion of brief quotations in a review.

ISBN: 978-0-9863112-0-8 (digital)
ISBN: 978-0-9863112-1-5 (paperback)

Book Website:

FastMuscleBook.com

All brand names and product names used in this book are trademarks, registered trademarks, or trade names of their respective holders.

Publisher:

Strategic Edge Innovations Publishing
340 S Lemon Ave #2027
Walnut, California 91789-2706
(866) 467-9090

StrategicEdgeInnovations.com

Book design, cover and editing:
Eric D. Groleau — EricDGroleau.com

Photo Credits:

Kellie Davis — motherfitness.com

Rob "Rage" Thompson — bit.ly/robrage

DollarPhotoClub — dollarphotoclub.com

Feedback and Suggestions?
Errors or Mistakes?

Send them to support@fastmusclebook.com

PRAISE FOR COACH ROB REGISH

"I've used A LOT of different training methods over the years but nothing compared to the results I saw with this."

—**Frank Castle**

****

"With regards to the Blueprint: It is definitely not just another program. It is very different from everything I have seen from the 'popular programs' crowd because it tuned and tweaked to lead into repeated states of borderline-overtraining and then to cut back on training stress just in the right moment in order to have the optimal growth stimulus. The addition of a strong adaptogen then fortifies and speeds up recuperation and regeneration tremendously, allowing for some insane gains within relatively short periods of time."

—**Dr. P** (Online supplement forum)

****

"Thumbs up for The Blueprint…. Everything you've heard is true and then some.

I have tried several lifting programs before, usually with mixed results. I came across 'The Blueprint' one day and started reading about it. I started reading every review I could find. I did not find one negative review, and many were gushing about the program.

I started reading it, and I had never even heard of some of the things he was talking about. Like the various stages the body can be in and how to manipulate the stages to your advantage, as well as the ways of finding out which state your body is in and when it has changed states.

Needless to say, I was pretty excited to start. I decided to spend some money on the supplements he recommended for those wanting supplements. (Note that this is not a supplement-based program. Supplements are not necessary, although taking them at the right dosage and the right times will roughly double your gains—at no time does he tell you supplementation is needed). I followed the instructions to the 'T.'"

I started out at 214 lbs and 17.2% Bodyfat. 1st stage ended and I was at 206.5 lbs and 15.5% Bodyfat. I am currently about 3 weeks into the 2nd stage of my first BP run and I am up to 222 lbs and my Bodyfat is at 16.1%. A quick check of the math shows that LBM has gone from 177.19lbs to 186.26lbs, or a gain of 9.07 lbs of LBM. Fat weight has gone from 36.81 lbs to 35.74 lbs or a loss of 1.07 lbs of bodyfat.

Conventional wisdom says that is impossible unless you are using steroids. Conventional wisdom is wrong, I hate to say. There is a substance that actually outperforms steroids in the long term (scientifically proven through numerous studies), and as the BP says 'The people have the ammunition, but they aren't pulling the trigger' regarding the use of this substance, which only works in certain stages and only after certain other things are done.

Now for the best part. When I first started, I was squatting 380 lbs 5 or 6 times and was struggling to do it. My 4th workout in the BP I hit 415 lbs for 4 reps, which was a PR for me. My 6th workout, I obliterated my PR 4 consecutive sets. That is not a mistype or misprint. I did 415 lbs x 8 reps/425 x 6 reps/435 x 6 reps/445 x 6 reps. My squat has gone up 65 lbs in 4 weeks. 65 pounds in 4 weeks!!

I could really care less if you believe this, don't believe it or think this is all a bunch of baloney. The results are real and so are the noticeable changes, which include my traps literally exploding although I have not done a single trap specific exercise since starting the blueprint, added thickness that has been noticed and commented on by others who see me on a regular basis (including a guy at work who works out and asked me what the hell I was doing to gain that size in that short of a time), and leg muscles that are growing in size and definition ... oh yeah, the best part is that *you likely will be working out less than what you are right now, as I am on a 1 on/2 off split to allow maximum muscle growth.*

Not only that, but I can tell you that Rob gives the best support of anyone I have ever seen. You can call/text/email/PM the guy and he responds very quickly. You can even request a customized program from him for a very low cost as well, but with the base program working so well for me, I doubt I will ever need one.

Bottom line is, I believe this program to be worth its weight in gold. With the new 3.0 version he has really outdone himself, including supplementation guide, a very detailed overview that is almost 80 pages long, trackers you can use on a daily basis that do a lot of the manual calculations for you, and workouts from start to finish. I cannot recommend this strongly enough. If he priced this at 10 times the price it's at now, it would still be a bargain. Imagine never having to try the 'supplement of the month' again and waste money, imagine never having to keep trying to figure out how to gain muscle and what to do (and not to do just as importantly).

You also get the exclusive 'Formula,' a workout drink so good I will never train without it ever again in my life, and very likely playing a big part in what has been happening, and the 'Recipe,' something new for 3.0 that will make your head spin.

Basically, all can say is that if you are tired of wasting your time and money and want to put on big time muscle over and over again ... do yourself a favor and follow this program, you will not be disappointed, I promise you—this is the truth!"

—***MATTER203*** *(Bodybuilding Forum)*

****

"Value: 10/10. You probably get the best after-sale service ever when you buy this, and the gains are repeatable per blueprint cycle.

Product effectiveness: 10/10. It's awesome, I put on a good bit of lean mass thanks to this program helping to put my body into an anabolic state.

Overall: 10/10. I can see myself doing blueprint cycles even a year from now.

The only thing I can say negative is I was told all I would need is 'A minimal level of equipment that provides progressive resistance.' I think that's a bit misleading because if you workout at home let's say and all you have is dumbbells, well then you're not going to get as much out of the program compared to someone that has access to much more than that."

—**DaCookie** (Online review)

****

"The strength gains so far are sick. I had high expectations but so far The Blueprint has surpassed them."

—**Canlhas**

****

"I am still trying to wrap my head around the progress I have made just from the famine period to present.

My bodyfat is literally melting away. Today was the 2–3 rep range for the feast phase. I surprised myself yet again and am proud to say I destroyed all my previous PR's."

—**Savabrat** (The Blueprint Collective forums)

****

"I have been a subscriber to the Blueprint Bulletin for over a year now.

Here is what I like:
- The information relates to diet and exercise and is current.
- The information can be read in less than 20 minutes.
- The information is back up with science.

All the above for the slightly higher cost of a bodybuilding, or men's magazine, that is filled with out-dated information and advertising from your latest peddler of protein powder.

This to me is far better value and well worth the cost.

Plus

With The Blueprint's latest offers, you will get lots of free goodies that could enhance your body to a new level of muscle or fitness.

Considering I was only going to subscribe for 3–6 months and it has now been a year shows that I find the information of true value and one that should be considered as part of your exercise equipment."

—**Rob Robertson,** Scotland UK

****

"Definitely the best money I've EVER invested!"

—**A. Perschbacher,** Blueprint Believer, Clinton, IN

****

"As a full-time strength coach I'm always looking for an edge to help my athletes perform at a higher level. This is why I subscribe to The Blueprint Bulletin. Rob Regish keeps me up to date with the newest training methods, diet strategies and supplement breakthroughs that can't be found anywhere else.

If you're going to stay one step ahead of your competition, subscribing to The Blueprint Bulletin is a necessity…"

—**Gareth Denyer,** Woodlands, TX, CPT, HCP Barbell

****

"Hello, I have finished the first week of feast and I don't know if this is magic or what. Although I have not gained any muscle mass (at least enough to be seen), I have gotten so much stronger. I feel stronger and I feel better. I work a summer job of bailing hay and lifting them felt like feathers. I look forward to finishing this and I wanted to thank you for the help in the progress I've gained so far."

—Joshua Bost

****

"My life has been forever changed. Most other sources of bodybuilding information regurgitate the same basic knowledge. But what I found in the blueprints and the bulletin was different from everything else out there. In the blueprints, Rob Regish spills the beans and provides much of what he's learned from years and years of training.

Every time I think that I've scoured the Internet to find all the beneficial supplements, the Blueprint bulletin comes out and blows my mind. In the bulletin, Rob Regish usually provides several overviews of the latest, as well as the old-school, supplements that one could consider. But he's not a bro, and tells his readers which ones they should not take as well as those that they should take. He's not even selling these supplements. In fact, many of his best recommendations are inexpensive, easy-to-find items."

—Sean Hynes

****

"I have gained 8 pounds in the last two weeks and I can guaran-freaking-tee you it ain't fat!"

—Tim G., Blueprint Believer, Louisville, KY

****

CONTENTS

Warning xvii
Acknowledgements xix
Foreword xxiii
Introduction xxv
Book Bonuses xxvii

15 Bodybuilding Secrets to Grow Drug-Free Lean Muscle Mass

TIP # 1: The Farmers Walk 1
TIP # 2: Another Win for Loaded Stretching 7
TIP # 3: The Fab 5 Bodyweight Workout 13

Get Your FREE Introductory Issue 23

TIP # 4: Super Lifts 25
TIP # 5: Benefits of Wave Loading 33
TIP # 6: Hyperplasia Training 37

The Best Muscle Building/Fat Loss Shake Ever! 68

TIP # 7: Abbreviated Training 43
TIP # 8: Pump Loading 53
TIP # 9: Building a Bigger Bench: The Setup 61

Get Your FREE Introductory issue 64

TIP #10: Stubborn Calves? 65
TIP #11: 5-Minute Pull-Ups, to Fix a Weak Back 69
TIP #12: Simplified Diet for Bodybuilding 73

Need to Lose FAT? 78

TIP #13: New Sarms On The Way 79
TIP #14: Three Pre-Workout Stacks 83
TIP #15: Overload Made Simple 87

Conclusion 91

Programs & Publications from Coach Rob Regish

The Blueprint Bulletin 94
The Blueprint for Big Muscle Building 101
The Blueprint Meteoric 107
Report: Progenadren 110
Report: Laxogenin 111
Report: Ultimate Relaxation 112
Report: Fast Fat Loss 113
Report: Ricochet Rabbit Fat Loss 114
Report: Neurobolt 115
Report: Protein Synthesis 116
Report: The Blueprint Mass Stack 117
The "Drink" - Build Muscle, Lose Fat... FAST! 118
The Hormone Optimization Course 119

Supplements Formulated by Coach Rob Regish

Progenadrex 123
MASS PRO Synthagen 129
TranQuilogen 137

About Coach Rob Regish 139

References: Next Steps 141

WARNING

The information presented in this book is not intended for the treatment or prevention of disease or any medical condition, nor as a substitute for medical treatment, nor as a substitute for medical advice. These statements have also not been evaluated by the Food and Drug Administration and the referenced food and supplements are not intended to treat, cure or prevent any disease.

This book is presented for informational and entertainment purposes only, and may not apply to your situation. Neither the author, publisher, distributor, RSR Fitness Systems, LLC, associated promotional websites nor any of their subsidiary companies, websites, personnel, publications or any media resource either known or unknown offer no warranty about the accuracy nor do they assume any liability to any party for any loss, damage, or disruption caused by errors or omissions, whether such errors or omissions result from negligence, accident, or any other cause. All links are for information purposes only and are not warranted for content, accuracy, or any other implied or explicit purpose.

The information contained herein reflects only the opinion of the author and is in no way considered required practice. Specific medical advice should be obtained from a licensed health-care practitioner PRIOR to employing the information which follows either in whole or in part, and before beginning ANY new diet, supplement, exercise or training program.

This book is meant to supplement, not replace, proper bodybuilding training. Like any sport involving speed, equipment, balance and environmental factors, bodybuilding poses some inherent risk. The authors and publisher advise readers to take full responsibility for their safety and know their limits. Before practicing the skills described in this book, be sure that your equipment is well maintained, and do not take risks beyond your level of experience, aptitude, training, and comfort level.

Undertake any of what follows, either in whole or in part, at your own risk.

ACKNOWLEDGEMENTS

Thank you to **John Drake, David Elliston, Eric D. Groleau, Reggie Johal** and **Carl Lanore**, you are the most incredibly talented, creative, kind, and generous people I have ever met. Working with you has changed my life.

The rest of the team at **Muscle and Sports Science**, as well as **Fusion Supplements**: Your dedication to sourcing the finest ingredients made my products even better.

Thank you to **Eric D. Groleau** for the beautiful design and cover of this book. Thank you too, for all the website work and dedication to making my dream come true. You are quite talented, and an absolute joy to work with.

No one is an expert in all things, including myself. When it came to a deeper dive on nutritional supplements, credit goes to **Adel Moussa** and **Sol Orwell** of **suppversity.com** and **examine.com** respectively. Thank you both so much for your generous support and excellent advice. Your expertise made an immeasurable difference.

I would like to thank my clients for their testimonials; the gift of their time and most generous comments; you allow those that don't yet know me to see me through your light.

Thank you to all my friends and family for their constant encouragement. To my late Gramma and Grampa, married for 70+ years!, for always believing in me—regardless of the goal. A life well lived, and an example for all of us to aspire to.

To my mentor and friend, Eddie Azzaro

Eddie took me under his wing in college, showed me how to powerlift. Through his selfless efforts, he took the time to show me how to train, eat and rest to realize my potential. He also stayed however long it took to answer my questions, and believed in me even when I did not.

Everyone should be so fortunate to have an Eddie in their life. At some point you should strive to return the favor, meaning mentor someone yourself once you're in that position.

A more rewarding experience you'll never have in life, I assure you.

God bless you Eddie, you gave me a gift beyond words...

FOREWORD

Rob Regish does something very few coaches do today. He cherry-picks what indisputably works best and assembles it into training programs which allows 100% of his clients to achieve their goals.

His training guides are to physical culture what individualized medicine is to healthcare. He's not striving to come up with a the next fad approach and attach his name to it. He strives to take what has worked and withstood the test of time, update it with what we know now, and provide a step-by-step approach to get you to your goals.

You'll never waste money reading his material. You will absolutely waste time and progress if you don't.

Best Regards,

Carl Lanore
SuperHumanRadio.com

INTRODUCTION

This book is the compilation of some of the best tips I've offered in the **BluePrint Power Hour** on <u>SuperHumanRadio.com</u>, via my monthly newsletter, **the *Blueprint Bulletin*,** and through many personal training consultations worldwide. It encompasses training, diet and drug details rarely discussed, and several of the ideas presented may strike you as "unorthodox."

It's worth noting that if you're doing something in the gym that runs contrary to what "most people" are doing, you're probably on the right track. Because "most people" get little to nothing in the way of results.

Thus, don't be like "most people!"

In many cases it's going to take a leap of faith, but it's well worth taking into consideration. What at first may sound contradictory will, in many cases, be the breakthrough you need. And please note that it isn't necessarily an either/or proposition. You may choose to "test" these techniques on your calves, for example (stubborn muscle group), or biceps, while deciding to leave the rest of your program intact.

On the supplements end of things, you're going to be reading about several concepts which might have been "unknowns" to you before. They are usually not available from national or heavily promoted brands. That's because they are from companies which have decided to put their money into the product, not advertising or doing "pro" endorsements! As for gray-market stuff, there will be some of that too.

By and large though, it's the ***training*** that drives this war. That's why you'll see most of the tips in this book are skewed in that direction. Otherwise, keep an open mind and consider giving these techniques a try.

You'll be ***real*** glad you did!

Yours in sport,

Coach Rob

PS - If you DO enjoy this book, please make sure you **leave a five-star review on Amazon** and download your bonuses at **www.FastMuscleBook.com**

This information is subjective.

Please keep this in mind when reviewing this book.

FREE BONUSES

As a token of appreciation for reading this book, you will receive a free copy of

The Blueprint Bulletin,

Fast Fat Loss - Special Report,

"The Drink" - Learn How to Make The Best Muscle Building/ Fat Loss Shake Ever!

Video Training Program.

Simply visit
FastMuscleBook.com
to register your book and
receive your GIFTS.

TIP #1

THE FARMERS WALK:
FOR CONDITIONING, FAT LOSS AND MUSCLE GROWTH—
HOW TO

From the Blueprint Bulletin
Volume 4, issue 12

Farmers Walks are "old school," but work better than virtually any alternative "finisher" out there. Whatever your game, they can be used to build up muscle, strip fat or any combination of the two. They are EXCELLENT at building work capacity, or the ability to do more work per unit of time. This translates into your next workout with barbells, dumbbells or bodyweight work.

TIES THAT BIND

Notice something about this guy? He's ripped, or at least VERY fit. He also carries respectable amounts of muscle tissue, the kind you need to hang on to a pair of heavy dumbbells or a trap bar, while walking challenging distances.

In terms of fat loss and conditioning, it's hard to beat. You could even make an argument that it out performs the sled and/or prowler, which is really saying something. Because in those two lifts, you're pushing or pulling a weight—not carrying it. Which isn't to say they're not BRUTAL—just birds of a different feather.

It seems carrying something heavy taxes you in a far more meaningful way.

And let's face it: Not everyone has a sled or especially a prowler. But everyone can grab a pair of heavy kettlebells, dumbbells or if you're so fortunate—a trap bar and WALK.

Sounds easy, but it ain't so easy!

FARMERS WALK VS. THE ALTERNATIVES: IT'S ALL UPSIDE

The nice part about Farmer's Walks is that they don't cause QUITE the oxygen debt versus the sled or prowler. Which is NOT to say you won't be huffing and puffing. Trust me, with enough weight you for sure will be. Because you can breathe more easily compared to the two aforementioned exercises, you can use heavier loads for longer periods of time, AND recover faster between walks.

That's a BIG advantage over the other two, especially in building muscle and *stripping body fat*.

If you want oxygen debt fast, the prowler and sled are great. But if you want conditioning, more muscle and less fat—the Farmer's walk is far superior.

Since you're upright through the entire exercise, they're also very spine and joint friendly, something that can't be said of other size and strength builders.

MORE BANG FOR YOUR BUCK

The sled and prowler work primarily the legs and posterior chain, with secondary emphasis on the upper body musculature. In English, the Farmer's Walk works a LOT more muscle groups. Not only will your lower body get a great workout, but the loaded stretch put on your neck, traps, shoulders, pectorals, back and other muscles (never mind your abs!) is tremendous. The short version?

Hands down: You'll grow more muscle with the Farmer's walk.

THE NUTS AND BOLTS

You can use the Farmer's Walk for different goals. I'll sketch out a few of them here, including ballpark weights and rest periods appropriate for each.

SIZE AND STRENGTH, FAT LOSS SECONDARY

Grab some heavy dumbbells or a heavily loaded trap bar and walk for around 30 seconds, with around two minutes of rest between carries. Use wrist straps for these, as your grip will be a limiting factor. Start slow with just 3–5 trips, ultimately building up to 8–10.

PURE FAT LOSS

You're going to be using a lighter weight here, but walking for up to two minutes with 45 seconds of rest between walks. As with the above, start with just 3–5 trips, ultimately building up to 6–8.

Once you get the weight right, it doesn't take much. The short rest periods really are brutal, and your heart rate should really be jumping.

BUILDING MUSCLE/LOSING FAT (EVERYONE'S UTOPIA!)

Use a heavy weight (though not as heavy as in the first example) and walk for just one minute, with a minute between walks. This 1:1 work to rest ratio with the right weight strikes the right balance and leads to the dual muscle building/fat loss results so many are after. Start with just 3–5 trips, and build up to 10.

Once you reach the upper end of the number of trips (8–10), you'll be among the most finely conditioned athletes in your gym–but leaner, stronger and BIGGER.

A NOTE ON PLACEMENT

Farmers Walks are best placed LAST during a workout, otherwise known as a "finisher." Yes, you'll be fatigued from your heavy barbell, dumbbell or bodyweight work BUT—that's the idea. You really push your boundaries (and up your conditioning!) when doing these last.

FINAL WORD

I hope I've sold you on Farmer's Walks, they really are that good. One final note: They're also what I consider a "level 7" exercise: Meaning they cause you to move the body and weight through space simultaneously. When this happens, the brain is at a VERY high activation level, and muscle building/fat loss is most efficient.

Give these a shot, you will NOT be disappointed!

TIP #2

ANOTHER WIN FOR LOADED STRETCHING: MORE STRENGTH, MORE MUSCLE GROWTH

From the Blueprint Bulletin
Volume 4, issue 12

There was a study[1] published 22 years ago that showed exceedingly high levels of muscle growth. It blew the doors off of anything I've seen before or since. The growth was so profound, it could only be explained by hyperplasia, not simple muscle hypertrophy. The key? Loaded stretches! I further add to this growth through the incorporation of Kaatsu training. Use this technique on a muscle group such as arms or calves for one month, with at least a month off.

WHAT'S IN IT FOR YOU

To most trainees, stretching is about the last thing they want to do, never mind between sets! Yet what if I told you that in addition to increasing flexibility, it increases strength[2] for your next set and growth too? And we're not talking a bit of increased growth, we're talking at least DOUBLING it.

Now, I've reviewed a LOT of papers on how muscles grow faster. But here's a shocker: Out of all the papers I've read the most incredible was from a study I saw a LONG time ago (1993). The author of that paper was Dr. Jose Antonio. You will often see Dr. Antonio's name in sports nutrition journals and some training related works. Through a very unique approach to stretching,

---

1 Antonio, J. and W.J. Gonyea, Role of muscle fiber hypertrophy and hyperplasia in intermittently stretched avian muscle. Journal of applied physiology, 1993. 74 (4): p. 1893-8.
2 Silva, J.E., Rauch, J., Lowery, R.P., and Wilson, J.M. (2014) Weighted Post-Set Stretching Increases Skeletal Muscle Hypertrophy. National Strength and Conditioning Conference, Las Vegas Nevada.

he induced some pretty jaw-dropping levels of growth in animals. Subsequent research at the University of Tampa has put a finer point on optimizing this technique.

It'll blow your mind, and muscles up…

HOW YOUR MUSCLES GROW —HYPERPLASIA STYLE

When muscles grow, they do so one of two ways. Either by making existing muscle fiber bigger (hypertrophy), or through the addition of new muscle fibers. It's the second method that I find FAR more exciting. Dr. Antonio's research was primarily centered on hyperplasia, which is gutsy, in my opinion.

There are two speculated ways in which animals/people achieve hyperplasia. The first is when existing muscle fibers split, and the second is when your body activates something called satellite cells. The satellite cells then divide and combine to form new muscle fibers. Both require extreme levels of stress to achieve their goal.

STRETCH OVERLOAD

Intermittent stretch overload is a technique that uses weights to stretch the muscle intensely, followed by rest.

Animal research has shown this type of training can still result in up to 50 percent increases in muscle size when the weight is not progressed, and up to 225 percent when weight is progressively increased.

Doubling your muscle growth isn't bad, but what if you could do even better?

Enter, Kaatsu training.

KAATSU

In this technique, you use small bands placed just below the knees or on top of the biceps to restrict (but not cut off!) blood supply.

So no necrosis for you, OK? Necrosis = BAD!

What the Japanese researcher found was that by doing so, there was an extreme buildup of growth factors in the muscle, leading to (much) greater muscle growth—using light weights. More muscle growth than seen in guys doing heavy training!

PRACTICAL APPLICATION

OK, here we go…

We're going to use two movements: The standing calf raise and the seated calf raise (the latter used to stretch the muscle only). By combining both techniques, I've found you only need to perform this workout once a week, twice a week max—and you'll achieve outstanding results!

First, before you get going—place a band just below each knee. The Nike or Under Armour arm band works for most guys, but I've found an ACE bandage or elbow sleeve folded over works in a pinch.

Here's a visual on the arm bands usually sold in most sporting goods stores. You see NFL guys wearing them a lot too.

Photo: Wrestler Rob "Rage" Thompson

Once you've occluded the muscle, set the weight on the standing calf raise to where you can comfortably get 25 or so reps.

Immediately after performing this set, hop on the seated calf raise with roughly half the weight you use on standing calf raises, and stretch the muscle for 30 seconds.

Now, rest 30 seconds and repeat four times your first workout, ultimately building up to 6–10 sets with progressively heavier weights in the stretch position only. What you'll find is that the first set of standing calf raises/

stretches isn't so bad, the second set gets uncomfortable and from the third set on, it gets intense. You should be feeling a pronounced burn during those standing calf raises, and your reps will naturally drop from set to set.

Here's how you'll know when to "cut it"—your reps drop to 15 or under. A drop of 10 reps or more signifies you've delivered the goods.

As you progress from session to session though, you'll find your work capacity increasing. Meaning you'll be able to perform more total sets before dropping to 15 reps or under. This is a sure sign the muscle is growing, and you should take starting calf measurements to verify—every three weeks thereafter.

SUPPLEMENTATION FOR RECOVERY AND GROWTH

This is an intense technique, and any attempt toward hyperplasia needs serious supplementation to support it. **Hyperplasia techniques are not without risk:** Elevated creatine kinase levels can result. Creatine kinase is a marker for muscle damage. In layman's terms, you can break down too much muscle—overwhelming your kidney's ability to excrete the torn up, damaged tissue. It's a lot more prevalent than you think, as any blood test for such will validate. Needless to say, using Synthagen and/or Progenadrex is highly recommended…

WHAT THESE PRODUCTS DO FOR YOU

Using Synthagen prior to, during and after the workout can help mitigate this damage—one look at the reviews as to how it wipes out delayed onset muscle soreness (DOMS) and accelerates recovery will attest to this. "Liquid Gold in a Bottle" as one of a dozen reviewers put it.

With respect to Progenadrex, literally every review has given it five stars. "Laxogenin done right," and a whole lot more I might add—Gains of a pound a week for 6–8 weeks (or more) are frequently reported. It gets even better: Virtually none of the weight gain is on the waist. You read that right, virtually everything is gained in the muscles!

TIP #3

THE FAB 5 BODYWEIGHT WORKOUT: HOW TO TRIGGER GROWTH, QUICKLY AND SAFELY

From the Blueprint Bulletin
Volume 4, issue 7

THE NEED

Nothing happens without overload, nothing.

If there's no "demand" for muscles to grow. They won't. Simple as that. No matter how many grams of protein you shovel down your gullet, how much creatine you take or how many "NO2'" caps you had today—it won't work.

THE USUAL FIX

The usual fix others and I prescribe is to up both your one rep max (alpha) and total tonnage (beta) strength. In other words, get stronger.

Various methods are used from loading patterns, to high-intensity training (HIT), Escalating Density Training (EDT), etc., but they all suffer from one or more flaws. They're usually LONG workouts, and even when properly performed, they take a LOT out of you. Moreover, the constant drone of heavy barbell/dumbbell work can result in chronic injuries.

No matter how good your form, how robust your joints are, etc., time has a way of catching up with you. Sooner or later, you'll need a better solution.

Which brings us to…

SOMETHING NEW

Wouldn't it be nice to overload your muscles in 15 minutes, do so with less insult to tendons, ligaments, etc. and gain some conditioning to boot? Yeah, I thought so!

So I'm debuting the Thinking Man's Bodyweight Workout: With Metabolic Conditioning. I call it **The Fab 5**, and you will too after you see what it can do for you.

GREAT STUFF, RARELY USED

Many of you know just how big I am on this bodyweight stuff. I usually point out all its advantages, people see the logic and agree it's a great concept. Six weeks later when I ask them how it's going—they never tried it!

I've finally figured out why most people ditch it: They're unwilling to buy books, like Paul "Coach" Wade's <u>Convict Conditioning</u> or Brooks Kubick's <u>Dinosaur Bodyweight Training</u>, and/or they can't cobble together a program they can live with. That's what I've been told anyway. Most are worried it will interfere with their weight training. Well, worry no more.

The Fab 5 workout is going to give you an easy entry point into the world of bodyweight training, and you'll see some pretty darn impressive results too. In most cases, those results are going to happen *fast*…

THE FAB 5

What follows is a bodyweight workout using only five moves. It works the *entire* body and will have you in and out of the gym in 15 minutes or less (after warmups). Yes, you heard that right—15 minutes or less to trigger some insane muscle growth, without the corresponding trauma of hundreds of extra pounds on your shoulders, back, etc. And oh, you'll be one well-conditioned ***beast*** when you're done with this too.

Without further ado, here are the five exercises you'll rifle through—then we'll get into the particulars:

- **Close-grip, palms up chin-ups (or pronated grip)**
- **Close-grip, elbows in pushups**
- **Bodyweight squats**
- **Hanging leg raises to parallel**
- **Bridges**

TRAINING FREQUENCY AND OTHER NOTES

You can train once a week using this workout, or whenever you're feeling the need to shake things up. In terms of recovery I've found most men and women can train productively again from 4–10 days later, as the neural adaptations/conditioning starts to erode after that.

These exercises are performed back-to-back, with no rest in between. Upon completion of one round, you rest 90 seconds and repeat for up to three rounds

IF and WHEN your conditioning improves. Why not four or more rounds? Because we're after INTENSITY, not VOLUME OR FREQUENCY.

Trust me on this, the conditioning alone you'll get from this workout is enormous. Before we go there though, I want to break down each exercise to explain why I hand-picked these five movements, and what each one will do for you.

CLOSE-GRIP CHIN-UPS

1–2 reps shy of failure
GOAL: 20 repetitions

The biggest, "baddest" and BEST bicep builder on the planet is the humble chin-up. First, that's because it works the biceps through two joints: Origin and Insertion (shoulder/elbow). You literally can't name a curl that does the same, and even if you could it still wouldn't trump the chin-up's ability to fire up the central nervous system (CNS).

Muscle is activated maximally when the body and weight move through space simultaneously. You won't find that with any kind of curl.

Obviously, you get other benefits too. Your lats will grow, your spine is naturally realigned and the abs get some fantastic static contraction work.

There are few athletes in most gyms that can perform 20 chin-ups without a lot of body English. Resolve to be one of them.

A slight "kink" in the arm at the bottom of the movement is preferred, as it keeps pressure on the muscle vs. jerking a tendon, etc. Also, a brief pause to establish your chin being above the bar is wise. Keeps people honest, and should prevent excessive body English (kipping).

Example: bit.ly/CGChinUp

The best part of this movement is this: It lights up your central nervous system like a Christmas tree, setting the table for what follows.

Which brings us to…

NARROW (NOT CLOSE) GRIP PUSHUPS

1–2 reps shy of failure
GOAL: 50–100 reps

If ever there was an exercise to pair with chin-ups, its pushups. There's a reason they're used in every military academy in the world, and been performed from the beginning of time: they WORK!

Unlike the bench press, pushups empower and invigorate the entire body. It demands muscle group engagement from the toes to the nose, and like the chin-up the abs must contract statically to stabilize the body.

Thumbs should be about a foot apart and elbows in, which is the form I'd suggest working with. In addition to building power, it's also the safest position the body will assume when pushing something.

If you're worried about the "high reps won't build muscle" mantra here, don't be. I've built up to 100 and gotten plenty of size for my efforts. If you insist though, elevating your feet onto a bench, keeping one foot in the air or the one arm pushups are acceptable alternatives.

They'll certainly bring your rep range down, LOL.

Example: bit.ly/NGChinUp

One final note: unlike the chin-up above, a rapid cadence is acceptable here. That is, I see no need to lock the elbows out at the top of the movement. The objective is to keep tension in the muscle, not in the joints.

BODYWEIGHT SQUATS

1–2 reps shy of failure
GOAL: 100 reps

Bodyweight squats are the quintessential "perfect" exercise. Brooks Kubick, in his excellent book *Dinosaur Bodyweight Training* recommends doing some variation of them every day of your life—with good reason.

These squats stimulate growth over your entire body, keep tendons, cartilage and knees strong and stimulate the metabolism—just like their barbell brothers.

Unlike traditional squats though, there is no loading of the spine or worries about the knees tracking inward as the weighs get heavier, etc.

THE FAB 5 BODYWEIGHT WORKOUT

Of all the exercises in this series, nothing takes more guts than to power through 100 of these—rapid-fire style. By that, I mean using a fast tempo—without locking your knees out and keeping the tension on the muscle. Most trainees gas out at 30, or the burning/cramping gets too intense even earlier!

In time though, you'll be shocked at how quickly your body responds, and you'll have the century mark mastered. You'll find few people who can keep up with you in most gyms at that level, doubly so after having gone through some intense chin-up/pushup work prior.

Example: bit.ly/BWSquat

HANGING LEG RAISES

1–2 reps shy of failure
GOAL: 20 reps

The hanging leg raise to parallel with a brief pause at the top, to demonstrate control, is the gold standard in developing the midsection.

They blow crunches, sit-ups, etc., out of the water for a number of reasons, but take my word for it: By the time you can do 20 letter perfect reps in this baby, you'll have stronger abs than 99% of gym goers around the world.

It looks deceptively simple, right? Wrong. I thought so too when I first tried these. You need a LOT of hamstring flexibility, hip flexor strength/flexibility (notoriously weak/stiff, in male athletes) and of course, abs of steel to pull this off with control. And that really is the key here, performing the exercise under total control—with no "swinging" or rocking allowed.

Are there more difficult abs exercises, requiring more strength? Sure. We can add clockwise/counter clockwise foot circles to this, perform the V raise with a plate on the lap or point the feet to the ceiling, but why bother?

The day you can do one or multiple sets of 20 hanging leg raises means you've arrived. And I can tell you from experience, it's not easy to get there!

FULL BRIDGES

1–2 reps shy of failure
GOAL: 1 set of 10

We finish with the bridge, which works nearly every muscle in your body. *Convict Conditioning* and several other books speak about the bridge being the ultimate exercise/the one they'd do if they could only do ONE movement, etc. I don't know about that, but I do know it's the perfect exercise to end the Fab 5 series with, and I tried many.

For what it's worth, I don't advocate quite the arch this young lady is using. I simply feel that if you can look behind you and see something upside down, you've done your job.

A word of warning on this specific exercise: you NEED to warm up thoroughly, before even attempting it.

After those 20 reps of hanging leg raises are done, you can imagine how tense your abs are. What you can't imagine is how GOOD it feels to stretch them out (indeed, virtually EVERY muscle on the front of the body), by bridging!

There are athletes that can perform 10 or more reps easily in this exercise, God bless you. The problem is that the cumulative fatigue at this point is overwhelming, so one sets of 10 reps is quite the benchmark for most people.

Example: bit.ly/CCFBridges

BOTTOM LINE

Many will look at the Fab 5 and dismiss it out of hand. Before you do though, do yourself a favor and TRY it! As a change of pace, I'm betting you'll LOVE what it does not just for your body—but your mind too. By covering the entire body so intensely, in such a short time frame, it really is invigorating. It's also completely scalable. Meaning athletes of all ability levels can use easier or more difficult exercise variations to suit their own tastes.

Remember, whichever variation you choose, the key is PROGRESSION. The next time you repeat this workout, you absolutely MUST get more repetitions than you did previously. Alternatively, you can add rounds as your conditioning improves. And that really is the true beauty of it: There are SO many ways to progress with the Fab 5, it boggles the mind.

Already achieved the 50 pushups with ease? Great. Switch to pushups with feet elevated, or one arm pushups. That'll add intensity and for sure get you in a lower rep bracket.

If you ever want to be inspired by what bodyweight athletes can achieve — You do NOT want to miss this video. If I hadn't seen it, I wouldn't have believed it! bit.ly/FitWorld

Want more muscle building tips?

Download your Your
FREE Blueprint Bulletin
introductory issue now at

www.FastMuscleBook.com

to accelerate your transformation!

TIP #4

SUPER LIFTS

From the Blueprint Bulletin
Volume 3, Issue 11

So your back aches, maybe even your knees. Perhaps you're bored with squats, deadlifts and step ups or you just need a break from all that vertical loading of the spine. You've heard me speak in glowing terms about the IronMind Hip Belt Squat and loading pin, but money is tight. (You're saving up to be a Blueprint Army GOLD member.)

No problem, I have your solution right here…

Part 1:
The Barbell Glute Bridge

WHAT IT WORKS

The barbell glute bridge works everything from your calves to your quadriceps/hams, glutes and as you can imagine, abs and lower back.

The thing I like best about it is this:

You can use a prodigious amount of weight, thereby building muscle and keeping in touch with the heavy iron—even with a bad back.

WHY IT WORKS

There are precious few movements that train the posterior chain in unison. Of those that do, they're nearly all of the standing variety. If an injury occurs, you're usually told the best choice of action is the reverse hyperextension. That trains the posterior chain and with no vertical loading of the spine, but your gym doesn't have one. And if you thought the Hip Belt was expensive, a home model Reverse Hyper would send you into orbit!

The barbell glute bridge works because…

- It trains the entire posterior chain, and then some.
- You can use enormous weights, stimulating muscle growth.
- You can do all of this, with virtually ZERO risks to your back.

Photo courtesy of Kellie Davie, MotherFitness.com

HOW TO EXECUTE

Load an Olympic barbell with a 45 lbs on each side. I've seen some heroes use 35s only to regret it later. You want 45s or at least something you can roll off your groin and legs.

Under no circumstances should you ever attempt to roll out over your head/neck. Seems obvious but I've seen it happen before—not pretty.

Place a "manpon" (those cylindrical pads placed around a weightlifting bar when squatting) around the center of the bar. If none is available, a thick towel will do.

Lie down with legs straight and roll the bar up to your groin. Now pull your feet up such that they're flat on the floor. I like having them as close to my bum as possible, just feels more powerful.

Grasp the bar with a medium grip, about what you'd use on a bench press. Now deep breath in and explode the weight upwards, holding it at its apex for a second before slowly lowering.

I personally feel there's much merit to going up on the toes, as the stress on the calves is magnified. What you'll find is that unless your setup is perfect, the bar has a tendency to wander and your hands are there to balance it. That's OK, just understand the setup is that crucial on this exercise.

Here's a good video/visual representation:
bit.ly/RGGluteBridge

PROGRESSION/LOADING

It's common in the early going to make 90 lbs jumps from set to set. Once past 405 lbs, I suggest resting a full 5 minutes between sets, to allow your central nervous system to recover. As the going gets tougher reduce jumps to 50, 25, even 10 lbs or less.

A good starting weight/rep spread is Bill Starr's 5x5. If you perform this movement once a week or even every 10 days, you're going to make some STAGGERING jumps.

It wasn't long before I was using 700 to 800 lbs in this exercise, and yes it'll attract some attention.

Women love asking about this exercise for obvious reasons, but in truth—it'll shape up her backside FAR faster than virtually any other method. And let's face it, most (but not all) women hate to squat or God forbid, deadlift. Many men I know also have a love/hate relationship with the squat.

Whether male or female, this exercise works and FAST. How fast? In six weeks I've seen it firm-up backsides that previously seemed hopeless. I've also seen it add a LOT to people's squats and deadlifts, when they do finally return to them. I have also noticed this generate a LOT of new muscle in the lower back/hams and calves in particular.

I mean really, how many other exercises can you move 700 to 800 lbs on? That's just me. I know several of you that put me to shame in the strength department, so you stand to benefit even more.

WRAP UP

This lift has been lost to the mists of history, much like pullovers. In terms of overload and how quickly it can change a physique, only the top range rack pull with static hold is even in the same league.

I'll also tell you this: If you've had trouble in the past building your calves, this exercise can work wonders. That's true, of course, if you're lifting the heel off the ground and you initiate the movement up, holding it there a second before lowering and your feet return flat—on the ground.

SCORECARD
(1 being the least, 10 being the most)

RISK OF INJURY: 1 (Maybe 2).

DIFFICULTY IN LEARNING: 2
— Movement will feel quite natural after a few attempts.

GROWTH POTENTIAL: 9
— Only thing missing is moving body/weight through space simultaneously.

UNORTHODOX FACTOR: 10
— People will stare, maybe ridicule. Sure sign you're doing something right.

Part 2:
Top Range Rack Pulls, With Static Hold

See this guy's back? That kind of muscle doesn't happen by accident. It's the result of years (likely decades) of vertical, horizontal and mixed plane rowing (i.e. T-bar rows).

In this forgotten lifts piece, I'm going to detail for you what I consider to be the ultimate physique hardening, central nervous system sharpening movement I've ever come across—The Top Range Rack Pull, With Static Hold.

Photo: Wrestler Rob "Rage" Thompson

WHAT IT WORKS

The better question might be, what doesn't it work? When I first proposed these, I took a LOT of heat for them. People claimed it was some kind of circus exercise, served no purpose, etc. Happy to say many of these same people are now converts, trumpeting the benefits of this movement.

This movement works every muscle from the back of your neck, right down to your Achilles tendon. It's not limited to the back of your body either. The shoulders, pecs, abs and quads are **heavily** involved. I consider it to be a full-body exercise, with the added benefit of lighting up the central nervous system like a Christmas tree and hardening the physique as good (if not better) than any other movement.

WHY IT WORKS

Overload, overload and more overload! What other movements can you handle 500, 600, 700 lbs or more in? Not many. Even then, how many of those movements were you able to hoist (with your hands) that kind of weight? Can't think of one. You can put more weight on the leg sled, maybe the top of the squat or use as much on the glute bridge—but the lower body is performing most of the work.

HOW TO EXECUTE

Bar placement is crucial. You want the bar to be at waist height, just enough such that when you grasp it, it moves an inch or two if you stand up straight. Speaking of grasping the bar, you want to take an overhand grip and use wrist straps.

The mixed grip as seen in deadlifting is problematic, in my opinion, and puts an unnatural strain on the palms up hand.

You for sure want to use wrist straps, and don't for a second feel bad about it because your grip will always be the limiting factor—given the amount of weight you can hoist.

Example: bit.ly/RackPullHold

Now, grasp the bar tightly and bending at the knees, dip under the bar. Stand up straight using the strength in your legs, back, etc., and simply hold it there until your static strength gives out. Two such holds for five seconds with a maximum weight, with at least five minutes of rest between holds (preferably 10 minutes or more).

Common errors: "Rolling" the shoulders in shrug-like fashion. Not using enough weight or performing the movement too frequently.

TRAINING FREQUENCY

This is one lift that takes a LOT out of you. Although the risk of injury is low (since the spine is largely straight up and down), you can't train this one too often! It's a lot like the deadlift in that regard. Ideally, you want to train this lift twice a month, three times at the most.

Those new to the movement may be able to get away with training it once every 10 days. Since your strength jumps so fast, that's quickly going to become twice a month. And that's how you should determine frequency: You should be making a 20, 50 even 90 lbs jump each time you train it. If you're not, you need to dial back the frequency!

PROGRESSION/LOADING

Unlike the glute bridge, this one doesn't lend itself well to a five sets of five protocol. Instead, work up to two static holds using a **maximum** weight, for five seconds. If you can hold it longer than this, up the weight until the hold time comes down to five seconds.

Take a minimum of five but up to **10 minutes or more of rest between holds is ideal**. The Russians rested for 20 minutes or more!

Why so long? In addition to your muscles being taxed, this lift demands a LOT from the central nervous system. Since the central nervous system recovers much slower than the adenosine triphosphate (ATP) and phosphocreatine (PC)/muscular system—you need more time. Both between sets and especially between workouts.

Also, adding 20, 50, 90 lbs or more as you get stronger, isn't uncommon.

SCORECARD

(1 being the least, 10 being the most)

RISK OF INJURY: 2 (Maybe 3)
—Just don't "twist" when you pull up on the bar.

DIFFICULTY IN LEARNING: 1
— Movement will feel quite natural. Feels like lifting a coffee table or couch.

GROWTH POTENTIAL: 9
— Only thing missing is moving body and weight through space simultaneously.

UNORTHODOX FACTOR: 9.5
— Not quite as "weird" as the glute bridge, but still draws curious looks. People will criticize you, tell you it won't work, etc. This is a great sign you're on to something big.

THE BOTTOM LINE

Perform this movement twice a month and train it heavy. If you do, it'll take you places you can only imagine!

TIP #5

Benefits of Wave Loading and a How-To Guide

From the Blueprint Bulletin
Volume 3, Issue 8

You don't hear much about wave loading anymore, and that really is a shame. It seems to go in and out of favor, yet it just may be what the Doctor ordered to get you to Gainsville.

Surprisingly, many trainees aren't aware of the benefits, so let's talk about that, then we'll get into some sample programs.

There are three big benefits when using wave loading: You can accelerate strength gains, increase your explosiveness and even your work capacity.

Accelerate strength gains: If your goal is to get bigger and stronger, you'll get there a lot faster vs. more traditional methods.

Step and wave loading are the two methods an athlete is most likely to successfully alternate. In *The Blueprint*, you have tons of step loading in the form of those six loading patterns. Adding wave loading is yet another arrow in your quiver.

Increase your explosiveness: If your goal is to improve the speed at which you move the load, there's no better training method. Provided you select the right weight and focus on speed of movement, wave loading will be VERY effective.

Increase your work capacity: The single dominant and common purpose of all wave loading is to exploit the principle of neural disinhibition. Meaning it helps to trick your mind AND body into lifting heavier weights, or be able to perform more reps at any given load.

The mind-muscle connection has several protective mechanisms intended to prevent you from hurting yourself. Wave loading, used judiciously, helps overcome these inhibitions and opens you up to a whole new world of performance.

SIMPLE WAVE

This should look familiar. It's how most people use wave loading.

- **10 reps of 225 lbs**
- **8 reps of 275 lbs**
- **6 reps of 315 lbs**
- **4 reps of 365 lbs**
- **3 reps of 385 lbs**

DOUBLE WAVE

What most trainees fail to realize is there's a GOLDEN opportunity to double up and be a LOT stronger the second time around. Let's look at an example.

- **10 reps of 225 lbs**
- **8 reps of 275 lbs**
- **6 reps of 315 lbs**
- **10 reps of 245 lbs**
- **8 reps of 295 lbs**
- **6 reps of 345 lbs**

Here you gain the added advantage of doubling your total tonnage, which for my money satisfies the amount of mechanical work necessary for hypertrophy.

The simple wave will get you strong, the double wave will get you strong AND big.

ADVANCED WAVE

You may or may not be familiar with Charles Poliquin's 1–6 training. It's a form of wave loading I like to employ after double waving:

- **6 reps with 275 lbs**
- **1 rep with 345 lbs**
- **6 reps with 280 lbs**
- **1 rep with 350 lbs**
- **6 reps with 285 lbs**
- **1 rep with 355 lbs**

BOTTOM LINE

Wave loading is best applied to your big barbell lifts such as the bench press, squat or deadlift. It's most effective for the trainee who's looking for size AND strength, vs. the loading patterns I prescribe in The Blueprint, which focus mostly on strength.

Right afterwards, I usually have you address hypertrophy with Escalating Density Training. And while that works incredibly well, a carefully crafted wave loading cycle is more "efficient." Meaning you'll get both in one shot.

Here's how I'd weave waves together, while strategically integrating a loading pattern. Assume we apply this to the squat...

THE SIMPLE WAVE
    (6 workouts) one week off
THE DOUBLE WAVE
    (6 workouts) one week off
THE ADVANCED/1–6 WAVE
    (6 workouts) one week off
GERMAN LOADING PATTERN (GLP) #1
    (6 workouts)

Once you complete the 1–6 wave, you'll have a reliable indicator of your one-repetition maximum (RM) and likely a lot more muscle.

This is the PERFECT time to finish off with German Loading Pattern #1, found in *The Blueprint 2.0*, *The Blueprint Meteoric* and it appears on the auto-calculator containing all six loading patterns.

I've seen trainees put on up to 20 lbs of lean body mass with this exact protocol, and emerge with a new personal record to boot. 24 workouts ain't a whole lot to sacrifice.

I like to think of it this way: You've got 24 more workouts coming anyway, why not give this a shot? Because if you're burned out on loading patterns, desire more hypertrophy or simply don't have the time for loading patterns + Escalating Density Training type workout, this simple/double/1–6/GLP #1 rotation is going to blow your mind.

TIP #6

HYPERPLASIA TRAINING: A HOW-TO GUIDE

From the Blueprint Bulletin
Volume 3, Issue 7

Hyperplasia is the recruitment of satellite cells under extreme stress that attach themselves to the existing muscle cells, thereby increasing the number of cell nuclei. Each nuclei added to a muscle cell increase the degree of protein synthesis that can take place. These are added permanently.

Ben Pakulski says something I found very insightful on this topic on his *Muscle Expert Interviews* podcast—if you have body parts that grow faster than others it is because those muscle cells contain more nuclei than a body part that doesn't respond as well.

So by applying the training protocol below you could potentially bring up lagging body parts by increasing the number of nuclei in the weaker body part's muscle cells.

In order to cause these satellite cells to attach themselves to the muscle cells require an immense amount of stress so be forewarned this is not a walk in the park—it hurts like hell while performing it and the delayed onset muscle soreness (DOMs) lasts for days after.

HYPERPLASIA OCCURS IN TWO WAYS:

1. Growth factors (IGF-1) trigger satellite cells to divide and fuse together to create a new fiber. This only occurs when a swollen muscle cell is placed in a stretched position.

2. Fiber splitting occurs when a muscle fiber reaches its maximum size—research has shown that the muscle fibers of bodybuilders are no larger than untrained people—they just have more fibers[3].

HOW TO DO IT

To implement it, you would perform a series of drop sets during your final set—after your regular sets have been completed. It is very important to have the working muscle fully pumped before starting the final set that will include the drop sets.

If you have done drop sets before this is nothing new. Where it differs is that between the last set and each drop set you will hold the weight in the fully stretched position for 20 seconds.

Once the 20 seconds have finished immediately grab the next weight and perform another drop set followed by another 20 second hold—continue till all drop sets are completed.

EXAMPLES USING FLYES:

After completing 3–4 sets of flyes with 60 seconds rest between sets, on your last set you would follow the protocol below. It is important to have a decent pump before doing the drop sets.

---

[3] MacDougall JD, Sale DG, Alway SE, Sutton JR: Muscle fiber numbers in biceps brachii in bodybuilders and control subjects. Journal of applied physiology: respiratory, environmental and exercise physiology 1984, 57:1399–1403.

HYPERPLASIA TRAINING: A HOW-TO GUIDE

1. **Final Set:** Pick a weight that you can just do height reps in perfect form (about 75% of RPM).

2. Tension must be kept on the working muscle at all times using a 4010 tempo.

3. After the 8th rep, hold the weight in the fully stretched position (bottom of the eccentric) for 20 seconds (30 seconds for advanced people).

4. **Drop Set 1:** As soon as the rest period has ended grab dumbbells with 20% less weight and do as many reps as possible (usually 5–8) with perfect form.

5. Tension must be kept on the working muscle at all times using a 4010 tempo.

6. Again, rest for 20 seconds in the fully stretched position while still holding the weight.

7. **Drop Set 2:** As soon as the rest period has ended, grab dumbbells with 20% less weight and do as many reps as possible (usually 5–8) with perfect form.

8. Tension must be kept on the working muscle at all times using a 4010 tempo.

9. Again, rest in the fully stretched position while still holding the weight.

10. **Drop Set 3:** As soon as the rest period has ended grab dumbbells with 20% less weight and do as many reps as possible (usually 5–8) with perfect form.

11. Tension must be kept on the working muscle at all times using a 4010 tempo.

12. Again, rest in the fully stretched position while still holding the weight.

13. Do one more rep with the weight and you are done—not sure why this is necessary—but it was stressed as important.

So in this example, if 50 pounds was your 8 RPM, your drop set weights (each reduced by approx. 20%) would be:

- **Final Set: 50**
- **Drop Set 1: 40**
- **Drop Set 2: 30**
- **Drop Set 3: 20**

You should expect to get 5–8 reps in each drop set. The lactic acid buildup and the pump is incredible. This, combined with the stretch under tension is supposed to cause hyperplasia.

Another interesting point: Dr. Jacobs states in the podcast—he has done experiments with human muscle cells in a Petri dish—just adding lactic acid to the dish caused the muscle cell to swell and to grow larger. This could explain why blood flow restriction training works.

Does it work? Damned if I know for sure but I would suggest, though, that it does. It just may be the ticket, to you growing truly NEW muscle fibers and finally, hyperplasia.

Learn How to Make the Best Muscle Building/Fat Loss Shake Ever!

FREE access to my video training program:

"The Drink" - Learn How to Make The Best Muscle Building/ Fat Loss Shake Ever!

Simply visit
www.FastMuscleBook.com
to register your book and receive this GIFT!

TIP #7

ABBREVIATED TRAINING: JUST HOW BRIEFLY CAN YOU TRAIN, AND STILL MAKE GAINS?

From the Blueprint Bulletin
Volume 3, Issue 7

Arthur Jones, the foremost proponent of High Intensity Training (HIT) in the U.S. His legacy and work was carried on by Mike Mentzer, and today by Pete Sisco of Static Contraction Training fame.

THE PREMISE

In the 1970s, Arnold was on top and volume training was all the rage. Everybody was bombing and blitzing with 20, 30 sometimes more sets per body part! Hours and hours were devoted to such pursuits, and just look at Arnold for the proof—it works! Or does it?

When Arthur Jones burst onto the scene, he carried a contrarian message that was as revolutionary as it was stark: **One set to absolute muscular failure was needed to stimulate muscle growth/hypertrophy.**

This was seen as a borderline act of defiance, but Jones was no dummy. He backed up his assertions with a real-life example and made a convincing argument. And, of course, he benefited monetarily via his line of Nautilus equipment.

Jones was among the first to realize a salient truth: You can work out hard or you can work out long, but you can't do both. It begged the question though, just how brief was brief with this new method? What it lacked in volume it more than made up for in intensity, but being a sport of extremes—people wanted to know.

What's important to understand is this: a productive workout can stimulate growth with just one "work" set, if taken to absolute muscular failure. Radical idea, so let's put it to the test…

TRAINING UNDER MENTZER

I was fortunate enough to consult with Mike Mentzer, former professional bodybuilder and carrying the torch Jones gave him. Mike was riding a wave of popularity due to then Mr. Olympia, Dorian Yates. His H.I.T. books, tapes, etc., were being pushed by Muscle Media too, which at the time was red hot and THE source of go-to information.

Upon discussing things with Mike, it became clear the man practiced what he preached: Most workouts consisted of 3–5 exercises at most, and all of them to gut wrenching failure. I can recall bench presses being supersetting with pullovers, plenty of squats, deadlifts and other exercises that worked the major muscle groups. Mike didn't mess around with the small stuff. There was no side cable laterals, etc. and on that score we agreed—waste of time.

Upper body movements were limited to 6–10 reps, lower body a bit higher—10–15 in some cases. Contrary to popular belief though, the workouts weren't too brief. Because once you work up using the really heavy stuff, it took a LOT of warming up to get there. I recall squatting with 450 lbs and let's face it nobody in their right mind would jump into that cold.

What blew my mind was the time off Mike recommended between workouts. What began as a 1 ON/2 OFF quickly went to 1 ON/3 OFF and eventually WEEKS went by in order for my body to heal and grow stronger.

Did it work? For awhile yes. Was it the best/most efficient way to go about things? Not likely. You start sweating the night before, you can't sleep. You get a bad feeling in your gut just thinking about the deadlifts you need to crank out, because you won't get another shot for a month. Last time I banged out

425 for 8 reps, tomorrow it needs to be 9 or more. You were quivering on rep 7 and where 8 came from nobody knows.

You get the picture. Ain't easy to top yourself EVERY time you step in there.

There was no magic to Mike's HIT. It was as he described in his books and articles. Only the rest between workouts would shock you, and it was too much for the average trainee.

LIFE GETS IN THE WAY

As you pass from your 20s into your 30s, life starts to get busy. The demands of work, marriage, a mortgage and a family weight on you. As much as you love it, training often has to take a back seat. There are bills to pay, mouths to feed and other responsibilities that need to be met. Still, you want great results from your training.

Is that really possible? And how LITTLE exercise do you really need to make progress?

I'm here to tell you, it can be done. There are a few qualifiers though, so let's discuss them. This may very well be the tipping point that allows you to train, gain AND have a life outside the gym...

YOU'RE SICK OF COMPLICATED PLANS

As good as it is, The Blueprint's dedicated Famine/Feast/Cruise protocol takes work—and LOTS of it. It's not just the gym work, it's the planning. You'll look like General Patton with all your graphs, charts, supplements, etc., and while there's a time and a place for that, some people need a break.

Yep, even me the guy who dreamed all this up needs a break. I'm guessing you do too from time to time.

QUALIFIERS

What follows assumes the trainee has around 10 years under the iron is well past the newbie stage and exploited the squat and deadlift to their maximum potential. That's a big assumption, but the resulting muscle/central nervous system is the "base" from which we will work. No base, forget abbreviated training. You need to pay dues before entering, but fortunately most have.

HOW BRIEF IS BRIEF?

Frequency

I would suggest that training twice a week is not only do-able, it's optimal for most males north of age 35. Fact is, marathon gym workouts and gym attendance records mean nothing. We've all been there, and it puts the body into a state of over-training. Plenty of muscle growth being stimulated, very little recovery and growth taking place. Moving to a twice a week training frequency will be just what the doctor ordered for many.

Volume

For most, 2–4 work sets will be plenty. Some may even be able to get away with one set to absolute muscular failure, though I wouldn't recommend it. For upper body movements, a rep range of 3–10 reps is preferred, allowing you to cycle between the upper and lower part of the range. And although you'll hear otherwise elsewhere, I feel strongly the same holds true for your lower body too. In fact, I think anything more than eight reps for hamstrings is a waste. More on that later.

Intensity

Forget one set to absolute muscular failure. It's not sustainable, at least for any length of time. Even if it was, the wear and tear on your muscles, joints, ligaments and especially your adrenals is too much. Instead, I look to lift more weight for a certain rep range.

Let's look at an example:

- **A workout devoted to 3 sets of 7**
- **A workout devoted to 2 sets of 5**
- **A workout devoted to 1 set of 3**

You see this rep range? I's pure GOLD when it comes to making progress. It needn't be 7's, 5's and 3's by the way, they're just examples. What's important is that they rotate, and the body can't adapt to them.

Whatever rep range you pick, remember this: of all the variables the body adapts to the quickest, it's REPS. In highly conditioned athletes, it can happen in as little as SIX workouts.

Second point: set volume should decrease, as the weights get heavier. This is important, as it'll allow you to focus more on pouring yourself into the heavier and heavier weights. Again, the 3 sets/2 sets/1 set protocol is just an example. You may thrive on something higher, perhaps 7 work sets, 5 sets and 3. The point being whatever number of sets you pick, make sure it decreases as the weights increase.

Training this way allows for less wear and tear on the joints, tendons and ligaments while staying in touch with the heavy stuff. Meaning your central nervous system gets just enough work to stay "sharp" on days when you're performing just three reps. You do NOT want to live there though, as doing so would lead to central nervous system burnout. The solution is simple: Return to 7 reps and dial up the set volume again.

SPLIT

If you're training twice a week, it makes sense to split the body up. Here, I favor a push/pull of sorts with the following arrangement:

DAY 1

- One arm pushups with weight held behind my back for three sets of 7.

- One arm dumbbell rows for three sets of 7.
- One arm barbell jammer press for three sets of 7.
- Chin ups, for three sets of 7.

DAY 2

- Box squats for three sets of 7 reps.
- Romanian Deadlifts for three sets of 7 reps.

Weighted hyperextensions, for three sets of 7 reps hanging leg raises to parallel, for three sets of 7 reps (hold weight between feet, if necessary).

The next time you perform this workout, you'd use the same exercise arrangement but perform two set of 5 reps per movement.

The final workout in the series is just one work set, for three reps in each exercise. It should go without saying that the weights used should be heavier. These workouts are considerably shorter, but that's the point—they take advantage of the tapering effect to radically boost strength.

Note also the thought behind each exercise. One arm pushups train the body unilaterally, ensuring balance. Barbell jammer press is much the same, albeit lending itself more toward heavier loading. The rows encompass both a horizontal row for the thickness (one arm dumbbell row) and a vertical row (chins) for width.

STATIC HOLDS

Without getting carried away, static holds can add a LOT to abbreviated training templates like this. Let's say you have a lagging body part, like calves. No problem, simply include the following at the conclusion of Day 2:

Seated calf raise: Load that sucker up with as much weight as possible, press up on the ball of your foot and HOLD it in the fully contracted position, for just five seconds. Two such holds with at least five minutes of rest between each hold, gets you to the grocery store.

Arms? I'd suggest strapping a dumbbell around your waist, taking a palms up or pronated (palms facing each other) grip and holding your chin above a chin-up bar for just five seconds. Once your static strength gives out, slowly lower yourself and exploit the negative.

The technique delivers stunning overload to the muscle groups in question, adds just a minute or two more to each workout but results in INCREDIBLE size, strength and hardness. Especially for the time invested!

COMMENTARY

I'm sure many here are scoffing at the low volume, lack of direct arm work, etc. Don't be fooled. These movements are incredibly demanding, work a LARGE amount of muscle tissue and fine-tune the central nervous system for absurd strength gains.

Because the rep ranges are constantly changing, there's no need to wreck your body by having to train to absolute muscular failure each session. In fact, you need only add 2.5 lbs (or less) on any given exercise, for the same number of reps.

While that may not sound like much, you'd be surprised how fast it snowballs. You wind up making progress virtually EVERY workout, with little to no adrenal burnout and healthy tendons/ligaments. The same CANNOT be said, for many a competing system.

EXPECTATIONS

So what to expect from something like this? Provided you met the qualifiers I spoke of earlier, here's what you're in for:

- Forget just keeping what you've got, you're going to get a LOT stronger.
- If concerned more with strength, look to perform each movement by itself (don't superset it), and rest a minimum of three minutes between sets.

- I personally follow the strength template. While I haven't seen much mass gain (not my goal), I've seen some of the most mind-blowing strength gains of my life.
- Expect to look back and cherish not just the strength gains, but the healthy joints/tendons and ligaments too.
- Unless you're keeping track of your #'s, it won't register how much progress you're really making. The mind is a fickle thing, so WRITE IT DOWN.
- As I stated earlier, adding small amounts to each rep range every workout adds up. Just how much over a few months is going to shock you.
- You look forward to your training. In fact, you CRAVE it. This is a HUGE sign, and I can't say it enough: If you're dreading your next gym visit, something needs to change. No other system I'm aware of gives you long-term sustainability like this.
- For those seeking more size/mass gains, the template can be "tweaked" by working with a slightly higher set volume/rep range.
- If that's your goal, consider structuring the exercises in escalating density training (EDT) fashion by "super setting" each movement, and resting just two minutes between each superset.
- You'll also want to increase the set total when training for size, shooting for as many as 5–7 upper body supersets, and 2–3 for the lower body. Since the lower body movements are more demanding, you need to limit the total volume of work, to preserve intensity.
- Might not sound like much, but try it and see—absolutely brutal. Not tough enough? Increase the weight, you'll see...
- Size gains are closely correlated with a certain threshold of mechanical loading, or work done per unit of time. By super-setting the exercises and adding additional work sets, you'll stand a far better chance of tripping that threshold.
- You'll notice I don't waste a lot of time on smaller muscle groups. Your mileage may vary, but I find if you're pushing/pulling on the compound movements and doing those justice—you get plenty of direct arm work.

SUPPLEMENTING FOR ABBREVIATED TRAINING: KEEPING IT SIMPLE

Part of the beauty of abbreviated training is that it isn't very supplement-heavy. In fact, I see only two applications that warrant including supplements, and neither is mandatory:

PRE-WORKOUTS & INTRA-WORKOUTS/ RESTORATIVE AGENTS

My reasoning is simple. Pre-workouts work as indirect anabolic agents, meaning they can (and do) result in a momentary increase in voluntary strength. The Ephedrine/Caffeine stack is famous for this, resulting in as much as a 15% increase in muscle contractile force. The more overload you can generate, the greater the growth signal.

That's just part of the picture though, recovery is the next step (with growth not far behind). Growth is simply a function of giving the muscle the TIME necessary to rebuild larger and stronger. And since we're only training twice a week, they'll be plenty of that. And it's free!

Which brings us to recovery. The faster you recover from these sessions, the quicker you'll grow muscle and be able to repeat the process.

You probably know I consider Synthagen the pinnacle of this, but I'm going to give you some alternatives to keep things fresh.

PRE-WORKOUTS

Our preferred solution here is NOT a thermogenic, as many confuse the two. Thermogenics are designed to burn more body fat/boost metabolism. Pre-workouts I consider a different category: They should reliably boost momentary strength, to lift heavier weights/move more weight per unit of time.

To that end, consider the following:

- **30 mg of Ephedrine HCL** — bit.ly/EPH40
- **300 mg of Caffeine** — bit.ly/JetAlert
- **1500 mg of Alpha GPC** — bit.ly/ALPHAGPC

We're pulling out the big guns here, which hopefully you've come to expect. Health-n-Vitality's Ephedrine is top notch, and if you order two 100 tab bottles, you get their buffered caffeine for free. (Throw my name in the discount code/referral section. Can't hurt and might land you some additional freebies.)

That little combo reliably boosts your ability to contract a LOT of muscle. How do we improve upon that? Glad you asked...

Alpha-GPC is a precursor to the neurotransmitter acetylcholine. Clinically, it's been used both orally and intramuscularly to treat Alzheimer's disease as well as to improve memory, cognitive function, and learning.

Choline (precursor to alpha-GPC) has been tested on athletes and shown to improve athletic performance and endurance. How does it work? Bright minds speculate acetylcholine is a major neurotransmitter that activates muscle contraction. Increasing the amount of acetylcholine (which is depleted by exercise) therefore keep muscles contracting longer and harder.

However, alpha-GPC is a much better precursor to acetylcholine and, unlike choline, alpha-GPC raises growth hormone (GH) levels substantially. I don't know about the GH angle. What I do know is that it NOTICEABLY and RELIABLY increase your strength. And it does so even more than things like phenyl-piracetam.

I suggest getting it on an empty stomach. If you do—pure GOLD.

TIP #8

Pump Loading: New Technique for Radical Muscle Growth

From the Blueprint Bulletin
Volume 3, Issue 3

There's a new method in town that takes advantage of something called pump loading and it promises to force growth—the likes of which you've never experienced before.

Here's the 10,000 ft overview:

- Pre-load the bloodstream with specialized anabolic and insulinogenic supplements.
- Pump and keep pumping these nutrients into pre-activated muscle.
- Activate and stimulate fast-twitch fibers while in this state.
- Induce, through specific techniques, supramaximal intramuscular pump volume, further engorging muscle.

Let's look at a practical example:

30 minutes prior to the workout, begin sipping the following drink to "pre-load" the muscles with anabolic/insulinogenic supplements:

- 50 grams of Karbolyn, or something like Waxy Maize/high molecular weight modified starches.
- 6 grams of citrulline malate.
- 3 grams of creatine monohydrate.
- 8 caps of Synthagen.

Continue to sip on this drink between sets, to continually "top off" these nutrients in your bloodstream.

Once these are in your system, your muscles will be flooded with nutrients to:

1. **Fuel these demanding workouts,**
2. **Speed recovery and**
3. **Fuel growth!**

Now, on to the workouts.

WORKOUT SCHEDULE

Monday: Legs — Heavy
Tuesday: Chest - Shoulders — Heavy
Wednesday: OFF
Thursday: Back — Heavy
Friday: Chest — Shoulders — Pump
Saturday: Arms — Pump
Sunday: OFF

Note this is a HIGH frequency program, but you'll find the workouts intense and FAST.

Like any other type of warfare, you get in, take care of business and get out of Dodge!

HOW AND WHY IT WORKS

Under normal circumstances, training doesn't force this much blood (and nutrients) into muscles.

However, when rest periods and rep ranges are brought down this low blood is pushed into muscle cells at a frightening rate.

When you initiate another set so soon, the muscle can't "flush" the blood/water out in time, and a "build up" effect takes place.

PUMP LOADING

The same goes for the supplements. Normally, they enter and exit the muscle cell in pace with the blood volume. Since blood becomes "trapped" inside the muscle—so do the carbs (water), citrulline malate, creatine and amino acids, etc. This is a GREAT thing, because it literally FORCES the muscle to expand like a water balloon.

Although the effect is temporary (during and immediately after the workout), the high frequency of these sessions causes the body to recognize it as "permanent," and muscle size follows.

You'll find you hold your pump a LOT longer too, from this type of training. It's usually gone within the hour, but it's not unusual to hold it for a good part of the day. Then, the next day you're right back at it—hammering another muscle group and getting the message across.

A second serving of "the drink" can be consumed immediately post workout but it's not entirely mandatory. Still, getting 100 grams of carbs in peri-workout (during workouts) is HIGHLY advantageous and you'd be wise to experiment with it!

THE WORKOUT

MONDAY

1—Leg Curl

Goal: Pump your hams—engorge the muscle with blood.
Sets: Four work sets (one minute between sets).
Reps: Eight rhythmic, pump type reps.

2—Speed Squats

Goal: Explosive reps. Drive up as hard as you can.
Sets: Six work sets (one minute between sets).
Reps: Six explosive reps (drive up as hard as you can).

3—Leg Press

Goal: Extreme pump to deliver nutrients and trap growth factors in the muscle. The more blood the better.
Sets: Five sets (one minute rest between sets).
Reps: 15 reps per set.

TUESDAY

1—Decline Dumbbell Press

Goal: Start with a dumbbell movement to get some blood flowing and get ready for the explosive work.
Sets: Four work sets (one minute between sets).
Reps: Eight smooth, full-range reps.

2—Bench Press

Goal: Explosive reps. Drive up as hard as you can.
Sets: Eight work sets (45 seconds rest between sets).
Reps: Five explosive reps. Drive up as hard as you can.

3—Incline Barbell Press

Goal: Constant tension with a tough weight.
Sets: Six work sets (one minute rest between sets).
Reps: Six constant tension reps.

WEDNESDAY
OFF

THURSDAY

1—One-Arm Barbell Row

Demo: bit.ly/OneArmRow
Goal: Constant tension with a tough weight.
Sets: Six work sets (90 seconds between sets).
Reps: Eight smooth, full-range reps.

2—Upright Rows

Goal: Explosive reps. Drive up as hard as you can.
Sets: Four work sets (one minute rest between sets).
Reps: Six explosive reps. Drive up as hard as you can.

3—Bent Arm DB Pullover

Goal: Constant tension with a tough weight.
Sets: Five work sets (one minute rest between sets).
Reps: 12 constant-tension reps.

4—DB Shrug

Goal: Blood flow and a pump in your traps.
Sets: Three work sets (one minute rest between sets).
Reps: 12 reps.

5—Speed Deadlifts

Goal: Pump to the entire backside.
Sets: Four work sets (90 seconds between sets).
Reps: Three explosive reps. Drive up as hard as you can.

FRIDAY

1—Seated Shoulder Press

Goal: Most massive pump you can get.
Sets: Six work sets (one minute rest between sets).
Reps: 12–15 reps.

2—Dips

Goal: Extreme pump to deliver nutrients and trap growth factors in the muscle.
Sets: Eight sets (45 seconds of between sets).
Reps: 10–12 reps to failure.

3—Dumbbell Bent Over Lateral Raise

Goal: Force and trap nutrient-filled blood in the muscles.
Sets: Four work sets (45 seconds between sets).
Reps: 15–20 reps.

4—Heavy Dumbbell Flyes

Goal: Maximal blood engorgement of chest muscles.
Sets: Five work sets (45 seconds rest between sets).
Reps: 8–10 reps.

SATURDAY

1A—Rope Pushdown

Goal: Maximal blood volume in triceps.
Sets: Four supersets each (no rest until Dumbbell Curl is completed).
Reps: 12–15 reps.

1B—Dumbbell Curl

Goal: Maximal blood volume in biceps.
Sets: Four supersets each (one minute in between each superset).
Reps: 12–15 reps.

2A—Barbell Curl

Goal: Force and trap nutrient-filled blood in the muscles.
Sets: Four sets (no rest until Dips are completed).
Reps: 12–15 reps.

2B—Dip Machine or Dip

Goal: Force and trap nutrient-filled blood in the muscles.
Sets: Four sets (45 seconds rest between supersets).
Reps: 12–15 reps.

SUNDAY
OFF

TIP #9

Building a Bigger Bench: The Setup

From the Blueprint Bulletin
Volume 3, Issue 2

There are a lot of loading patterns out there to boost your bench. We use these in The Blueprint to great effect, often putting 20, 30 or sometimes 50 lbs or more on during extended cycles. Yet, there comes a time when form and technique need to be torn down in order to progress further.

Looking at most trainees today, things start to go wrong in one critical area: The Setup.

You absolutely can't bench big without starting from a position of strength. This isn't talking down to anyone, I could use the help too. When taking an honest look at it, we can all do better. To that end, I'd offer this introspective look at your setup.

SIX STEPS TO SUCCESS

When you break a movement down and really analyze it, you arrive at smaller steps to work on. Such is the case with the setup. Although these fine points might look trivial and you're most likely following SOME of them. Getting ALL of them right makes a HUGE difference. Let's take a look…

Step 1: Tuck the feet underneath your body, NOT out in front!

The bench press is a full-body exercise. A LOT of that power is driven up through the legs. It's my opinion that this leg drive is most efficiently generated from a "tucked" position. If you're not already doing so, practice tucking the feet and driving from the toes. This will add anywhere from 10–30 lbs, just using this one tip.

Step 2: Practice the art of the bridge/high chest and belly

You want to keep the buttocks and shoulder blades on the bench, with the lower back arched and chest/belly high. The logic here is simple, the higher the bar touches, the less distance the bar has to travel. This adds another 10–20 lbs to your max lift!

Step 3: Push your toes into the floor and drive your shoulder blades into the bench

Now that your feet are tucked and your chest is up, dig those shoulder blades together and into the bench. Pressing from your toes seems to transfer the more power than pressing from the heels. This combination adds another 10–15 lbs to your top bench press.

Step 4: Grip the bar with a "death grip"

Squeeze the hell out of the bar. This will activate all muscle groups more effectively, but in particular the triceps. The triceps are an incredibly important part of the lift, with some authorities stating it's THE most important muscle group involved.

Step 5: Keep the bar in line with the wrists/elbows

One of the biggest mistakes you can make is to use what I call the "motorcycle grip." This is when the bar is cocked back in your hand, as opposed to inline with your wrist and forearm. When you DO get it in line, magic happens. People lose a LOT of power when they fail to observe this rule. It will feel uncomfortable at first, but practice, practice and practice some more.

Step 6: Set the bar at lockout

When you take the bar out of the rack, spend some time "setting" it. Waiting a few seconds will compress your elbows and traps and push you deeper into the bench. All that compression just locks your body in tighter, and a drop of 1–3 inches is observed. This means you have to move the bar that less further to lockout!

FINDING YOUR SWEET SPOT IN THE LOCKOUT

One of the BEST tips I can give is finding your most advantageous "lockout" position. This refers to where the bar should wind up when completing the lift. MANY a lifter loses the lift here, but with this tip you'll drive it home…

You want to begin with an empty bar, ideally on a free-standing bench. Once you lay down, hold the bar at arm's length. Next, slowly move the bar in an arc from a position behind your head to a position above your waist. Observe the tension/amount of muscular force needed to keep the bar from slipping out of the groove.

What you'll find is there's a point along this curve where the bar feels almost "weightless." PRESTO, you just found your optimal lockout position!

SUMMARY

Many of us practice a few of these tips, but few (including me) habitually nail ALL of them. Once you do, it's not uncommon to add 20, 30 or more lbs to your max bench! The key really does lie in the setup, and practicing these tips until they become second nature. Give these a shot. In conjunction with the various loading patterns we use in *The Blueprint*, there will be no stopping you from setting new personal records!

Want more muscle building tips?

Download your Your
FREE Blueprint Bulletin
introductory issue now at

www.FastMuscleBook.com

to accelerate your transformation!

TIP #10

STUBBORN CALVES? INTRODUCING THE KAATSU KNEELING CALF RAISE

From the Blueprint Bulletin
Volume 2, Issue 9

If you weren't born with 'em, you have to grow 'em. "Stubborn" calves are for real, and yours truly suffered from Small Calf Disease (SCD).

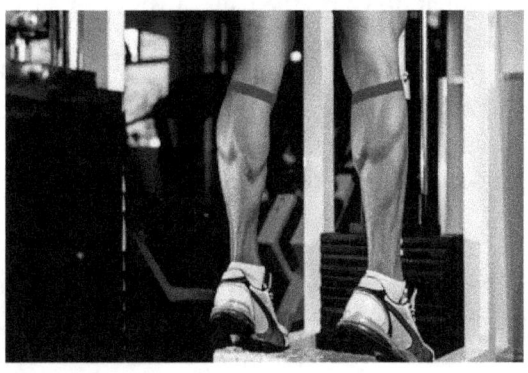

Where there's a will there's a way though, so let's talk solutions.

I'm from the school that calves get a lot of work just carrying your bodyweight around all day, and nothing less than an extreme stress is needed to stimulate growth.

Static holds are a fantastic solution, as are running in JumpSoles. However, each suffers from one fundamental flaw—you can't train them very often, given the stresses involved.

To really shake things up, consider the Kaatsu kneeling calf raise.

THE BASICS

I dreamed this up one day in the gym, although I'm sure someone else thought of it first.

To perform this exercise, you first occlude the calf by wrapping an ACE™ bandage just below the knee. You do NOT want to cut the blood supply off completely. Instead, you want to tighten it just enough to partially restrict blood flow. I use this method because studies show that two weeks of Kaatsu training increased muscle growth to a greater degree than five weeks of regular weight training. More on that in a bit.

Next, you want to squat down on the balls of your feet, just in front of a flat bench.

Place your hands on the bench for balance and lean forward. Pressing from the balls of your feet, perform calf raises from the floor and squeeze hard at the top. You're shooting for three sets of 33 reps with two minutes of rest between sets.

Finally, you do NOT take the wraps off between sets. Leave them on until you've completed all three sets.

TWO-WEEK BLITZ CYCLE

If your calf training has stagnated, consider a two-week blitz of this.

The guidelines are as follows:

- **Intensity is low, around 20% of your one-rep max. In this case, we're using just bodyweight.**
- **Training frequency is twice a day, six days per week.**
- **The minimum duration of Kaatsu training is two weeks, for a**

- **total of 24 sessions in 14 days.**
- **You must wait at least four hours between sessions**

If this sounds easy, think again. The searing pain has to be experienced to be believed. This is due to the metabolic buildup within the restricted muscles of lactic acid—which leads to an enormous increase in growth hormone.

Studies by Takarada[4] in the year 2000 showed training with vascular occlusion of the lower extremities resulted in a 290-fold increase in the plasma growth hormone. Compare that to what well-known researcher Richard Kraemer[5] found in 1990. In that study, trainees using 80% of their one-rep maximum for large muscle groups rested one minute between sets. They found just a 100-fold increase in growth hormone.

It's not even close!

BOTTOM LINE

This is an exercise you can perform anywhere, anytime. It requires no equipment and no gym—just guts—and a lot! I can honestly tell you that I've seen fantastic results in two weeks' time, and know you will too.

---

4 Rapid increase in plasma growth hormone after low-intensity resistance exercise with vascular. occlusion. Yudai Takarada, Yutaka Nakamura, Seiji Aruga, Tetuya Onda, Seiji Miyazaki and Naokata Ishii J Appl Physiol 88:61-65, 2000.
5 Hormonal and growth factor responses to heavy resistance exercise protocols. Kraemer WJ1, Marchitelli L, Gordon SE, Harman E, Dziados JE, Mello R, Frykman P, McCurry D, Fleck SJ.
J Appl Physiol (1985). 1990 Oct;69(4):1442-50.

TIP #11

5-MINUTE PULL-UPS, TO FIX A WEAK BACK

From the Blueprint Bulletin
Volume 5, Issue 1

WHY I'M WRITING ABOUT THESE METHODS?

I continue to get a lot of good feedback on my abbreviated training articles, because

1) They work and;
2) People are increasingly pinched for time.

And as I'm fond of hammering home, people need realistic solutions that generate muscle growth. Very, very few of us have the luxury of dedicating 2–3 hours/day or even a workout to our favorite pastime.

In truth, would you want to? That constitutes overtraining in all but the most advanced/enhanced athletes…

Pull-ups are the ultimate test of upper body pulling power.

You'll often find 250+ lbs bodybuilders or powerlifters who can't do a single pull-up, and this is as sure a sign of being "exposed" as there is… Unlike the bench press, squat and deadlift, repetitive training in this single lift will see it improving, not getting worse. There isn't the central nervous system disinhibition seen with the classical lifts, due to not strapping hundreds of extra pounds on the bar, joints, tendons and ligaments.

It's one of the few lifts where practice makes perfect.

PROGRAM POINTERS

- Don't use straps. Instead, use chalk as it'll REALLY build a better grip. This holds true even if you have a weak grip to start. You'll find that in 2–3 workouts, you develop a grip from hell…
- Don't go to failure. Instead, leave a rep or two in the tank for each pull-up variation.
- Your weakest pull-up should be first, meaning for most, a wide-grip, palms up variation.
- On your subsequent sets bring the hands just 1" closer together. You'll find you're fatiguing in this position, which is perfectly natural.
- After moving the hands in once, switch to an overhand palm grip.
- Once you've been through that iteration, switch to a supinated grip where the palms are facing you.
- Finish with a close, underhand grip, which is the strongest position for most trainees.
- Do NOT go to failure on any set. Instead, go 1–2 reps shy.
- Towards the end, you may be doing singles. Which is perfectly natural, and you should find yourself struggling with even these.
- Rest as long between sets as it takes you to do justice to the next set. For some, this will be as little as 10 seconds. For others, it'll be up to a minute.
- As you progress in the program though, you'll find you need to rest less between sets. This is an indication of increased strength/work capacity. It doesn't take long.

WHY IT WORKS

The primitive nature of the pull-up is what makes it a key movement in any training program. Pull-ups were once a necessity of life in evading predators and obtaining food sources (pulling up into a tree).

This has all be been lost in gyms today, as simple "high-tech" solutions like the "lateral pulldown" have been invented. Let's be clear about one thing: The lateral pulldown is a poor excuse to train your back. In fact in most cases, it'll hurt you more than it'll help you.

There's also this variable inherent therein:

You're moving the body and weight through space simultaneously. Whenever you do this, the brain and central nervous system are at a much higher acti-vation level. You activate a whole lot more muscle mass and stimulate more growth.

PROGRESSIONS

The classic approach is to just add reps. You can do this for a long time using this method. But there's another approach that'll get you even further. In fact, two...

1) Adding weight and;
2) Progressing to one arm, "uneven" pull-ups.

Of these two, I'd suggest uneven pull-ups as they build a hellacious grip, phenomenal lat development and a rock solid core. It's not unusual to be extremely sore in your abs during the following days. Part of the reason this method is used at most—twice a week.

Example of uneven chin-ups:
bit.ly/unevenpullup

You can see here where he has one hand around the wrist. This movement was popularized again in the "Rocky" movies and is making a comeback in most gyms. NOTE: You should be able to perform at least 10 close grip, palms up pull-ups using two hands before attempting 1–2 uneven pull-ups.

SUMMARY

Two 5-minute sessions every 7–10 days is all it takes. Who doesn't have 10 minutes? This is the ultimate in functional strength; it takes little to no time and will give you wings/lats to die for. Much better than popular "back" routines most trainees are using today.

TIP #12

Simplified Diet for Bodybuilding: Easy Calorie/Macro Splits, for Building Muscle

From the Blueprint Bulletin
Volume 5, Issue 1

In order to determine how much you need to eat, you need to know where you're at today. The maintenance caloric calculator I'll be providing here is simple and scary accurate. You also need to know where that extra weight is coming on.

Another simplified tool you can use every two weeks, to make adjustments if need be, is a tape measure. While most trainees have no idea as to how many calories they're eating nor how to track where the weight's going, they end up "sloppy" after a bulk.

Using the two simplified tools, you will be able to establish your baseline and diagnose every two weeks allowing you to "auto-correct" your diet based upon these two objective diagnostics.

There really is no simpler way to achieve your goals of putting on more muscle and less fat.

THE NEED

I often recommend establishing maintenance calories intake/protein requirements before setting up a diet. The problem is, most folks are just guessing. In order to put a finer point on that, I figured I'd write this article, to help make it easier for you to follow a meal plan to achieve your goals.

STEP 1:
THE MOST IMPORTANT FACTORS

The most important factors are the total calories and the macros. Many trainees continually adjust their calorie intake and macros, as well as other variables, to determine the best diet their body will react to. Finding the perfect nutrition plan for your body usually takes a lot of trial and error. A good nutrition plan must be tweaked over time because as you're building muscle and getting bigger—your calorie and protein needs will change. MOST trainees never take this into consideration.

Your body will take some time to adapt to a new food regimen so it's important not to change things too drastically, or too soon. Before you can come up with a nutrition plan, you need to know where you are at. It's important to find an accurate way to track your weight and body fat percentage. Weight alone will not tell you how you are doing and neither will body fat percentage, but when these two are combined, it will give you a relatively accurate way to track your fat mass and lean body mass.

THE DIAGNOSTICS

First, take your total bodyweight on a scale. This should be done first thing in the morning, after you've done your business in the bathroom, stripped completely naked. You do this once every two weeks. Not every day, not multiple times a day! Second, you're going to get a flexible tape measure. The kind they sell in the sewing department at most local dollar stores.

Every two weeks, you're going to measure:

    1) Your upper arm/bicep measurement (flexed) around thickest point.
    2) Your chest/back (around the nipples).
    3) Your waistline, around the belly button.
    4) Your legs, about halfway down.

I'd suggest adding 500 calories/day to your maintenance intake, ideally timed in the two hours post exercise or in the morning at breakfast, if you are not training that day. These totals almost 3,600 extra calories/week, which should equal one pound of lean body mass/muscle per week—this is a realistic rate for the drug-free trainee.

If every two weeks the tape measure is staying the same or making smaller circles around your waist, and your other measurements are making bigger circles OR your strength is going up, you're on the right track! If not, some adjustments will need to be made. Suggest cutting back on calories and/or carbs to stop the fat gain in the waist—if fat gain is your problem.

Really folks, it's that simple. The waistline measurement is the key.

STEP 2:
ESTABLISHING YOUR MAINTENANCE CALORIES FOR THE DAY

When designing your nutrition plan a good place to start would be to figure out how many calories it takes for you to sustain your current weight. Here is a great maintenance caloric calculator: bit.ly/mbfcaloriecalculator

To gain weight you would need to be above maintenance. A good place to start is 20 calories multiplied by bodyweight. So if you weigh 200 pounds, start with 4,000 calories. If your waist measurement isn't budging and don't see your muscular measurements going up enough after two weeks, you can up the calories. On the other hand, if you are putting on too much fat, you can reduce the calories a bit. The key is to check in every two weeks where you can auto-adjust, based upon your findings. This is something almost NOBODY else does, so take heed: It's one of the most powerful strategies available to you.

PROTEIN CONSUMPTION

The amount of protein you consume each day is secondary to the quantity of calories you eat. You'd think this was the opposite from reading bodybuilding magazines, but of course—they all sell protein supplements! Without enough protein, gaining muscle will be difficult. It's often said most people who are looking to gain muscle should be shooting to eat about 1-1.5 grams of protein per pound of bodyweight per day. I DO NOT agree with this, as it's really closer to one gram per pound of lean body mass (not bodyweight), that should determine your figure. So if you weigh 200 lbs and carry 175 lbs of muscle on your frame, you should take in around 175 grams of protein/day. More important than that is protein.

TIMING

You want to flood your body with free form Essential Amino Acids pre- and post-exercise, then feed it at least 25 grams of top-notch whey, milk and egg or beef protein right AFTER exercise. The easiest way to accomplish the former is Mass Pro Synthagen, which can be found here: bit.ly/synthagen

Otherwise, get your protein spread out over the rest of the day between five and seven small meals. The most critical time, though, is again intra- and post-workout. This, due to the fact your muscles are in a hyper-state of absorption due to being stretched/contracted under a load. They'll literally soak up the amino's like a sponge.

NOTE: If you're ordering Synthagen through Muscle Mass, you want to sign up for their free newsletter. They don't pepper you like other newsletters, but what you DO get are unadvertised specials on Synthagen and other items: bit.ly/MuscleMassSite and if you're in Europe, you can get it from Predator Nutrition: bit.ly/PredatorUK

CARBS

Carbs are also an important part for the muscle-building process. A lot of people focus on protein and neglect the carbs and wonder why they aren't packing on muscle. The majority of your calories come from carbs, especially when you're bulking up, around 2–3 grams of per pound of bodyweight. So that 200 pound trainee should be aiming for 400–600 grams/carbs per day.

NOTE: Slow-burning carbs, like quinoa and oatmeal, are a good start with your carb intake since this will raise glycogen levels, which increases your stored energy and discourages fat spillover.

The exception to this would be your morning meal and your post workout meal. Here you want simple carbs because they raise your insulin and help you to absorb nutrients like protein. That can be something as simple as a high glycemic juice, dextrose or an engineered carb like Pure Karbolyn.

Still have trouble gaining weight? Add more carbs, but focus on getting up to 50% of your daily total in the two-hour post-workout. Like protein, the muscle is sponge for carbs during and after training. It all goes back to glycogen synthase, the enzyme that stores carbs as glycogen in muscle. It's absolutely jumping during your training, so be sure to take advantage with this useful tip!

You'll be absolutely astounded at how these carbs don't "show" on you, vs. when consumed at other times of the day.

FATS

A lot of athletes forego dietary fats because they're high in calories and/or they believe they'll be deposited as body fat. It's not true! In fact, I went on a ZERO fat diet back in college. What happened? My strength tanked, my energy tanked and I felt and looked like crap. Your body NEEDS fats, in fact the essential fatty acids are just that—essential. You can get these from eating a fatty fish, like salmon, 2–3 times a week, or taking one tablespoon of a high dose fish oil/day.

You can also use a good quality supplement, like: ULTIMATE OMEGA World's #1 Omega-3. NON-GMO Nordic Naturals. Big 473 ml (96 serv.) bit.ly/AskMass

Now you also need to be eating some form of cholesterol, despite what the doctors will tell you. Reason? Cholesterol is the starter material for testosterone synthesis! Here's the chain of events. Cholesterol – Pregnenolone –

DHEA – androstenedione – 4 androstenediol – testosterone. No cholesterol, no Test. You can easily get "enough" by eating red meat a few days/week or by having eggs with your breakfast. Other good sources of fats include olives/olive oil, flaxseed oil, coconut oil/milk and mixed nuts.

SUMMARY

While a lot of this may not seem "ground breaking," the tools I've given you to work things out are. In particular, that calculator for determining maintenance intake and the tape measure. Almost everyone has a scale, and the cost of a tape measure is nominal. But how many people are using that tape measure, to see just where that extra weight is going? Virtually nobody. You put those tools into practice (along with the training tips I've dropped here and elsewhere) and I guarantee you'll be putting on muscle in short order.

Need to Lose Fat?

**Download my
Fast Fat Loss - Special Report
today at**

www.FastMuscleBook.com

FREE for readers of this book!

TIP #13

NEW SARMS ON THE WAY

From the Blueprint Bulletin
Volume 5, issue 1

SARM is short for Selective Androgen Receptor Modulator. Compounds dock at the steroid receptor site, but don't impart most of the classic side effects as steroids.

The early SARM's results have been disappointing (in terms of muscle building). Despite this, pharmaceutical companies continue to refine their research and seem to be chipping away at it. These new SARMs represent a potential step forward, for athletic performance enhancement purposes.

If you've followed my articles on SARM's, you'll see that I'm not very high on them. Most are too weak, down regulate your natural testosterone production and don't impart the "feel-good" properties that prescription testosterone does. That may be changing, as three new SARMs look particularly promising.

Although not commercially available yet as "research chemicals," you can bet they will be at some point. Thus, the heads up.

LG121071

The LG121071 SARM was developed by Ligand Pharmaceuticals. It's still hard for athletes to get hold of, but doping hunters have already developed a test for it. While the test hasn't been implemented yet, by the time you read this—it likely will be. In 1999 Ligand published a study in which they reported that LG121071 attaches just as well as DHT to the androgen receptor. Doses of 20 milligrams or more (orally) are likely needed in humans.

No research could be found to demonstrate androgen cell binding (nor prostate), but being a SARM—it has to work through at least the former mechanism. This is likely the next SARM you'll see on the market, as it's closer than the next two.

MY TAKE: I don't think this one is going to pan out. The need for such high dosage amounts isn't consistent with the SARMs which have shown promise so far. I'd table this one for now.

ACP-105

ACP-105 is produced in Sweden. It's not yet available in online stores, but yes like the SARM above—a doping test has already been developed for it. This SARM first appeared in the literature in 2009. The study showed that a relatively low concentration of it attaches to the androgen receptor better than DHT.

Quoting one of the studies: "The principal finding from this study was that 1 [ACP-105] produced a robust anabolic effect on the levator ani muscle (67% reversal of ORX-induced atrophy at 1 [mg/kg]/day) while having fewer androgenic effects on prostate (21% reversal; T, 48%)". The human equivalent of the dosage mentioned for a man weighing around 180 lbs would be circa 11 mg per day.

MY TAKE: This has more potential than LG121071, but falls into the same category—best to wait for more real world feedback, before buying any...

LGD-3303

I've saved the best for last: LGD-3303. The chemical structure resembles LGD-4033. Some who've used it say it's the most powerful SARM that an athlete can buy... LGD-3303 is not yet available (but I suspect it will be shortly). On paper, this particular SARM is head and shoulders above the other two. Could this be the breakthrough SARM we've all been waiting for? Only time will tell, but I've heard this story before so I'm still skeptical.

A dose of 1 mg per kg per day was sufficient to completely replace a person's natural testosterone production. The human equivalent dose for a man weighing around 180 is circa 11 mg per day. Further, an animal study published in Endocrinology suggests that quite unlike other SARMS, it has a prosexual effect. It even has the ability to apparently heighten libido in female rats!

MY TAKE: This one has potential, the best of the three. The low amount needed per day to replace a man's natural test production suggest it's POTENT. Although I couldn't find evidence for this, it suggests it might be suppressive though. Whether or not this risk versus reward profile is acceptable to you is an individual matter. Like the others, I'd suggest you wait on it awhile and follow the board feedback.

Overall, I see SARMs being refined into better and better iterations for performance enhancement, with the side effects being minimized. Something to keep your eye on in the future, but wanted to give you the heads up here first.

TIP #14

Three Pre-Workout, Focus and Concentration Stacks Not Currently For Sale – But Should Be: Your How-To Guide

From the Blueprint Bulletin
Volume 5, Issue 1

I'll be focusing here on nootropics and various other products that amplify the 'stimulate' part of the stimulate, recover and grow equation. Virtually all of these lead to more strength in the gym, or concentration in other endeavors.

PRE-WORKOUTS

A good pre-workout should increase your momentary ability to lift heavier weight, and do so for longer periods of time. The gold standard here was the ephedrine/caffeine stack. While that's still available if you know where to look (see my *Fast Fat Loss/Ricochet Rabbit Fat Loss* special reports), you have far more elegant solutions that are considerably effective.

Athletes with high blood pressure will also find this useful, and if you're not in the habit of taking yours–start. I don't think you should just live with high blood pressure, because you could very well die from it. These stacks are part of the solution.

The problem is that most "pre-packaged" formulas are little more than dressed up caffeine, some stimulatory amino acids, more caffeine and occasionally some yohimbe sprinkled in. This is anything but effective, and often work against you. Instead, we're going to head-on over to Powder City and put together some stunningly effective pre-workouts that optimize the mind/muscle connection without frying your central nervous system.

NOTE: All cocktails are to be taken on an empty stomach, approximately 30-45 minutes before training/activities requiring intense concentration.

PRE-WORKOUT FOCUS COCKTAIL #1

ADRAFINIL: 600 mg
  bit.ly/PCAdrafinil
CAFFEINE/THEANINE CAPSULES: 200 mg
  (400 mg optional, if stimulant effect is desired)
  bit.ly/PCCapsuleStack
ALPHA – GPC: 1 gram
  bit.ly/PCAlphaGPC

TIP: The Powder City discount code
"powders10" gets you 10% off!

COMMENTARY: Adrafinil is the pro-drug to Modafinil, which increases alertness, focus and concentration for several hours–with zero central nervous system stimulation. Some may find an additional boost desirable, and for this we layer in time tested caffeine along with a bit of L-Theanine (to prevent over-stimulation).

The addition of Alpha-GPC really puts this over the top, as the more acetylcholine available, the stronger the muscle contractions you can generate. The effect lasts a good six hours, so it is best taken earlier in the day to prevent disturbing your sleep.

PRE-WORKOUT FOCUS COCKTAIL #2

CAFFEINE: 100 - 200 mg
    bit.ly/PCCaffeine
TIANEPTINE: 25 mg
    bit.ly/PCPhenibut
PHENYL PIRACETAM: 100 mg
    bit.ly/PCPhenyl

COMMENTARY: Quite overlooked is Tianeptine's ability to amplify stimulants, something you wouldn't garner from the literature on such. However, it makes perfect sense once you read the glowing feedback about how it brightens your mood. Once the caffeine kicks in and happiness gets into full swing, a healthy dose of phenyl-piracetam delivers laser like focus for the task at hand.

This cocktail is fantastic before social gatherings where you need to be upbeat, sociable etc., but also excels pre-workout. It's the happiest of all stacks listed here.

PRE-WORKOUT FOCUS COCKTAIL #3

CAFFEINE/THEANINE: 200 - 400 mg
    bit.ly/PCCaffeine
ACETYL L CARNITINE: 1.5 grams
    bit.ly/PCALCAR
GALANTAMINE: 8 mg
    bit.ly/PCGalant

COMMENTARY: Here again we're boosting acetylcholine in the brain, including the driver caffeine - but this time prolonging the life of acetylcholine via galantamine. It does this by preventing its breakdown. This is a low stimulant, mega-focus pre training formula that'll make a noticeable difference on max day. It lasts a good 4 hours, washing out faster than pre-workout focus cocktail #1 but still a has a nice tail to it.

So there you have it folks, 3 surefire ways to fire up your brain/CNS to boost strength and work capacity pre-workout. Most of these are inexpensive and a hell of a lot healthier for you than ingesting high dose caffeine/yohimbe etc.

You need to remember: Over-stimulating your central nervous system/brain can be detrimental to strength instead of enhancing it.

TIP #15

Overload Made Simple: How to Magnify It

MUSCLE GROWTH IS A 3-STEP PROCESS:
1. Overload a muscle
2. Recover and
3. Grow

That's a fundamental, biological law that can't be circumvented. Given that, you'd be shocked at just how many people aren't achieving step 1. That's right, they're not even firing the gun. No overload, no stimulus to grow. Worse, recovery suffers because overtraining is prevalent and the trainee is left scratching their heads as to why they've hit a plateau. Is it any wonder performance-enhancing drugs are so popular?

Overload can be as simple as this: perform as many chin ups in five minutes as possible. Let's say you get 30 chins in five minutes. The next time you train, your sole objective is to get more than 30 reps. If you can't, you failed to stimulate growth. But if you do, you'll know with certainty that you did. You'll also have the satisfaction of knowing you got more done in five minutes than most trainees get in three hours of winging it.

There are several supplements that can magnify your efforts to overload the muscle. Micronized creatine monohydrate is probably the most cost effective. Due to greater ATP pools, creatine will allow you to get more reps. Likewise, beta-alanine acts as an intracellular buffer to extend the time muscle will contract before seizing up.

X-Factor (aka Arachadonic Acid) is superb addition here, as it amplifies the perceived damage to muscles after being incorporated into the cell membrane. Phosphate supplementation has also shown to be of benefit, upping your ability to move more weight in any given unit of time.

The amino acid L-Taurine and minerals zinc and magnesium play a crucial role. Taurine is among the finest amino you can use, especially for increasing blood flow. Typically, a 3–5 gram dose is ingested an hour prior to training. Zinc and Magnesium deficiencies are common especially in North America, and allow the muscle to keep firing for more reps. I'll caution you that getting the right forms is crucial.

Most store-bought magnesium and zinc are the **oxide** form. You might as well flush it down the toilet, your body can't absorb it. When supplementing these minerals you want the aspar**ate**, picolin**ate** or ci**trate** forms.

Next, we get to stimulants. There's no question the right amount can increase your momentary ability to contract muscle. The issue I have with most pre-workouts is this: most are laden with excessive caffeine or yohimbe, leading to an overstimulated feeling that can actually work against you. They're also overly expensive, and have absurd profit margins for supplement companies.

Instead, I highly recommend a low to moderate dose of ephedrine hydrochloride and caffeine. But ephedrine was banned, right? Nope, not if you know where to look. Where to look is behind the counter, at your local pharmacy. You want to ask for Primatene tabs, which by label include 12.5 mg of ephedrine HCL. You'll need to present your license and sign for it, but it's **well** worth the effort. While you're there, pick up some dirt cheap caffeine tabs. I like Wal-Mart's in house brand, "Jet Alert". In any case, you want to dose caffeine to ephedrine in a 10:1 ratio. In this case, you'd ingest 125 mg of caffeine an 12.5mg ephedrine (by label, Primatine is 12.5mg ephedrine hcl/pill). More seasoned lifters can titrate up to 250 mg caffeine and 25 mg of ephedrine, but I wouldn't go too much higher than that. The ideal is to be stimulated and not shaky, paranoid and sweating profusely. It's a fine line.

Finally, we get to select amino acids for strength. In this arena, I rather like Mucuna Pruriens and/or Alpha GPC. Mucuna Pruriens is now available in the form of 98% extract for L-dopa. That means a big dopamine rush, especially when tagging along with ephedrine/caffeine. Consider adding 150 mg to your E/C stack.

Alternatively Alpha GPC is a very, very sharp amino acid for strength. Research has demonstrated improvements in exercise performance, focus and even greater GH output when consuming it—pre-workout. It works by elevating levels of acetylcholine, a key neurotransmitter in muscle contraction. 600 to 1,200 mg pre-workout works exceptionally well. I've had some of my best workouts on this stuff, and highly recommend it.

And if you're looking for the ultimate in tunnel vision, consider Modafinil. Sure, it's a controlled substance but Adrafinil is not. It's the precursor to Modafinil, a non-stimulant medication used to keep people awake. Adrafinil takes longer to kick in (45 minutes), but a distinct focus improvement will be realized. If you have a big workout coming up or just want to see what these can do for you, I'd suggest dosing E/C and/or Alpha GPC and Adrafinil for ultimate focus.

Growing muscle all comes down to firing the gun though, and that means training. In future Blueprint Bulletins, I'll show you different ways of ensuring overload each and every time you set foot in the gym…

CONCLUSION

I hope you have enjoyed these tips but most importantly, I hope they have inspired you to take action towards achieving the results you're aiming for.

Nothing happens overnight but results do happen when people take action.

I believe these tips can accelerate your results and keep you motivated through the process. Some of them might be outside of your comfort zone and that's fine. They are definitely not essentials or absolute prerequisites to your success.

Most of these tips were published in my monthly Blueprint Bulletin publications. If you enjoyed them, please take a second to register your book to receive a free sample issue along with one of my special reports and a video training as my thank you for getting this book.

In the following pages, I have included some information about my other publications, programs and the supplements I have formulated. Make sure to visit my website regularly to stay on top of your game.

All the best on the road to "Gainsville"!

Coach Rob

PS - If you've enjoyed this book, please make sure to **leave a five-star review on Amazon** and download your bonuses at **www.FastMuscleBook.com**

PROGRAMS & PUBLICATIONS BY COACH ROB REGISH

The Blueprint Bulletin

The Biological Law, That Governs Muscle Growth

It's ALWAYS a 3-step process: Stimulate, Recover and Grow

Always, always, always. If you're a human being and you're interested in growing more muscle, you absolutely MUST pass through these three steps. If you don't, you won't grow any new muscle. Simple as that. Which brings us to what usually goes wrong first: People aren't even getting out of the starting blocks, because of conflicting information: They fail to perform even step 1. It's not your fault, it's part of a carefully orchestrated campaign to keep you frustrated, which we'll get to later.

For now, let's look at your training...

WHY YOUR GYM VISITS DON'T STIMULATE MUSCLE GROWTH

Let me give you an idea of what usually happens. Legions of young men sign up every year to build muscle and lose fat. For some it's to impress the girls, others want to excel on the athletic field. The motivation behind their decision isn't what matters. What matters is they made a decision to physically change. That's a good start, but nature requires something more—a lot more than just gym visits. The problem is this: Most people are just "winging it" in the gym.

The stimulus to build muscle has been known for over a hundred years—it's called overload. You demand more of the muscle than it's used to, give it enough time/food to repair and rebuild itself larger and stronger and ... presto! YOU get bigger and stronger! Seems like an easy prescription to follow, yes? Unfortunately, it's not. Part of that is due to the fact your body is an adaptive mechanism, and will stop responding to the same stimulus if you go to the well one too many times.

In advanced athletes, plateaus can occur in as little as SIX workouts!

Every month in The Blueprint Bulletin I detail a completely fresh, real-world example of how to stimulate muscle growth via a different overload techniques. And since the typical overload program could get you plateauing in 4–6 weeks, you'll KEEP getting these gems in your inbox every month—which means you'll KEEP GROWING. No more "guessing," no more "same old, same old." You'll get a tried and true method to stimulate muscle growth every 30 days.

How about the exercises themselves? Did you know there are some that are a complete waste of time, and others that build muscle at a phenomenal rate? Yet, droves of gym goers continue to randomly select the same old movements for their biceps, triceps, chest, etc. EVERY time they go to the gym! This is another reason you're not growing: Inefficient exercise selection. Let's look at an example...

In most gyms I visit, I see lots of guys curling their biceps into oblivion. Everyone wants big guns. I've seen standing barbell curls, incline DB curls, preacher curls, hammer curls and the real laugher—concentration curls. The fact is, "big arms" start with the triceps, as they contain two thirds of the upper arm mass. Regardless, let's get back to curls. As the 16th set drones on, our man is screaming in pain and satisfied with his "pump." More often than not, the pain is due to tendonitis from over-training and his pump will be gone in an hour. His biceps aren't getting any bigger either, in some cases they're getting smaller (due to over-training).

The fact of the matter is this: The best bicep builder in the world is the humble chin-up. The reasons are numerous (recall NMA from above), but it's also because it works the bicep from origin to insertion (shoulder to elbow)—something no curl movement can claim. Due to much greater NMA, it doesn't take 16 sets either. In fact, it takes a modicum of that to grow big guns—especially when you understand how to pair it with triceps work. The Blueprint Bulletin will show you how to load/de-load these superior movements for continuous, uninterrupted and explosive muscle growth.

Until you get this down all that extra protein you've been eating, all the creatine in the world, etc., won't do a darn thing. Once you DO get it down though, things start happening—and fast. Stop "winging it" in the gym and let The Blueprint Bulletin show you how to pull the trigger.

With fundamental #1 covered then, we turn our attention to…

DIET: WHY WHAT YOU'RE EATING ISN'T AS IMPORTANT AS WHEN YOU'RE EATING IT!

You know sugar is bad for you, so you try to stay away. But let's be honest: Do you keep track of every morsel of food you eat? I supposed all of us could, but would you really want to? Here's an even better question: Do you need to, in order to get results? How about all that protein you're pounding? You know, the old maxim of one gram of protein per pound of bodyweight—you've been doing that for years. The result, in most cases? Makes those protein powder companies a lot of $, and leaves you with a lot of gas.

Instead of focusing on this nonsense, macro nutrient timing is the key.

The Blueprint Bulletin shows you how, where and why timing is so important. You can kiss your love handles goodbye and say hello to bigger arms, quads and pecs with this information alone.

Stop obsessing over whether intermittent fasting, ketogenic, cycling ketogenic, low-fat, low carb or high protein diets are right for you. Until you get the timing down on when these macronutrients should be ingested, no diet in the world will put muscle on you.

There are plenty of diets that'll put fat on you though, that much is clear. It's often been said that It's a lot easier to eat an inch on to your waist vs. your biceps. And it's TRUE! Right here, right now—try this: Can you pinch more than an inch of fat around your midsection?

If you can, you've been taking in too many calories. The Blueprint Bulletin shows you how to rearrange these calories, such that food is preferentially re-partitioned toward muscle and away from fat.

SUPPLEMENTS: WHY 99% ARE A COMPLETE WASTE OF $$$

By far the #1 "solution" to your problems is offered up by companies in the form of supplements.

They're enticing, because…

- There's always a new one, with some outrageous claims behind it;
- They're readily available, shipped right to your door in most cases and;
- Don't require a lot of effort. Swallowing pills and powders usually doesn't…

The only problem with the supplement solution is this:
99% OF THEM DON'T WORK!!!

The big caveat, of course, is nothing works—unless you do!

Listen, I use them on a regular basis. So yes, I think there's some value in supplements.

But let's be honest: Do the results you get in most cases—justify the cost? If you're like most people, the answer is no!!!

Yet, you've been manipulated to KEEP pumping money into supplements every month because… there's a formula these companies use. The formula is predicated on your frustration, which is where this all began. You're not getting the results you want, and is it ever fast enough?

Fact is, there are a select few supplements that DO make a difference. When and where you use them though, is also important. Every month in The Blueprint Bulletin, you'll be given the 411 on what works, what doesn't and whether or not Product X is worth the $. You'll know with certainty what that 5% is, and get the straight dope (not the ad copy), on what it'll do for you.

This information alone can save you hundreds if not thousands of dollars in the course of a year.

HOW I KNOW THE BLUEPRINT BULLETIN IS RIGHT FOR YOU?

I know this because I've lived it. For over 30 years, I've scratched around looking for answers—answers that'll help solve your problems. You absolutely NEED this information to progress at the fastest possible rate. Put an end to all the training, diet and supplements lies right here, right now—for good.

Still not convinced? Consider the following:

Every issue addresses the Stimulate, Recover and Grow equation applying either training, dietary or supplement recommendations to each. If your current information resource isn't doing this, your plateau is virtually guaranteed to be permanent.

No vested interest: Outside of three products I formulate (all clearly identified), I have NO vested interest in the multitude of training systems, diet strategies, books/resources or supplements I review for you.

Researching this information by yourself would be a full-time job, even IF you knew where to look! Let someone do that work for you, because you have better things to do.

No other "authority" has such wide-ranging access to world class medical Dr's, labs, trainers, dieticians or supplement gurus as I do. Big claim but ask yourself: Where else have you heard things such as Buckminsterfullerine/C60? You don't…

The straight dope on what works, what doesn't and what to steer clear of in this field. And trust me—the list is LONG of those people/companies you do NOT want to do business with!

It would take you 30+ years to learn these lessons the hard way and accumulate this much knowledge. My desire to share it with you stems from a sincere desire to help people avoid the mistakes that I've made.

There are no pro-contracts or scholarships out there for me, at age 45. There may be for you. In fact, several Blueprint Bulletin subscribers have done just that—leveraged this information into scholarships or pro-contracts!

BOTTOM LINE

Invest TODAY in The Blueprint Bulletin, because the solution to your problems is just one-click away…

You'll be on the cutting edge, and receive your newsletter via email every month.

Everything's on the table…

- Training
- Diet
- Supplementation
- and unorthodox solutions I've found in the most curious of places!

This is a fantastic way to stay one step ahead of your competition, training partners and use these little-known gems to up your game.

While The Blueprint was and still is cutting edge in many respects—we live in the information age, and information doubles every 18 months.

You'll find this powerful information right here—each and every month to complement what you have learned with the Blueprint.

You'll be on the cutting edge, and receive your monthly issue via email at the end of every month.

THE BLUEPRINT FOR BIG MUSCLE BUILDING

Natural born, biologically perfect hormones designed for YOU, by YOU

What Makes The Blueprint Program Different?

It's the only training program that shows you how to grow muscle via Hyperplasia, something only demonstrated up until now in animals.

- Why hyperplasia is a game changer, and what supplements absolutely seal the deal when you put the Gray Market Supplement Guide into play.
- Why "typical" bodybuilding sets fail to stimulate hyperplasia, and how you can "tweak" things to grow absurd amounts of muscle–and fast.
- Why incomplete recovery between sets is the trigger that sets

- hyperplasia into motion, and the surprisingly affordable (and legal) dietary supplement that cuts intra-set recovery time in HALF.
- How the way you're training today virtually guarantees no new muscle will be grown—and how you can quickly rectify that situation to start piling slabs of new muscle on fast…
- Why eating this one macronutrient is a BAD idea post workout—slowing down the growth process and causing you to lose out on the most anabolic time of day…
- Going to non-functional: The precise physiological state you'll find yourself in, after completing the hyperplasia routines.
- Non-functional rebound: How to literally flood your body with key ingredients that quickly pull it out of non-functional and vault your physiology into muscle growth hyper-drive.
- And more, a LOT more!

Join me, in becoming one of the last Anabolic Outlaws. The type of people interested in building superhuman physiques legally, safely but with drug-like gains to show for it.

The New Blueprint 4.0 System Includes The Blueprint 2.0 and 3.0

The infamous steroid guru's figured this out and increasingly touted an array of anabolic drugs to force one's physiology into a state of rapid muscle building. So, is there a natural way to "steroid-like gains" in muscle mass and super strength without the bad risk-to-benefit ratio of bodybuilding drugs? YES, it really is possible. The Blueprint 2.0 will teach you the important Famine phase. The Blueprint 3.0 includes the caloric zigzags concept and further information on static holds.

The Blueprint 4.0 System Also Includes The Blueprint Meteoric

A repeating 8-week cycle that draws upon three different energy systems.

What does this mean? It means you'll get big, shredded and in record time. It would seem the body's adaptive response can be further amplified, given the careful arrangement of certain exercise, diet and supplementation fundamentals. It became clear for example, that what distinguished Blueprint 2.0 and 3.0 from any other training system was that the speed of methodical change was faster. Faster than any other program out there.

Is it REALLY possible?
YES, it really is possible...
Stick with me, I'll show YOU
exactly how it's done.

Let's talk about a way to generate the traction needed to pack on new, real muscle. Besides, it's not just your testosterone levels that are holding you back. Plenty of younger lifters are walking proof that having lots of gas in the tank and no GPS gets you nowhere, fast. What you really need is a GPS system in that Ferrari of yours! Like everyone, you have a physiological "blueprint" ready to grow heaps of muscle mass. That's right, there is a common mechanism by which your body can flood itself with Testosterone, Insulin, IGF-1 and other muscle building goodies...

Natural born, biologically perfect hormones designed for YOU, by YOU.

It's your personal BLUEPRINT
for BIG MUSCLE Building.

THE KEY is in understanding how to coax your body into a high state of "organic anabolism," and then knowing how to AMPLIFY and extend its duration. Before we go any further, please know that this is NOT some ultra-complicated system that requires a master's degree to apply. It's easy to learn, but you'll only find it here because I am the founding researcher and copyright holder.

In a nutshell…

I've stripped away all the junk to bring you THE TRUTH about muscle building and getting stronger at an alarming rate, CONTINUOUSLY.

The "Blueprint" is presented out in easy-to-follow steps that work in natural harmony like no other drug-free, organic bodybuilding system before. Best of all, it works over and over again, ongoing. Even seasoned pro-level athletes and former steroid users are reporting BIG GAINS with this NEW landmark bodybuilding course. Can you imagine your physique and strength gains after literally living in a state of biologically perfect organic anabolism for six weeks? How about six months? A year from today? Get ready to shock and awe a few people!

If you truly want to build honest muscle and get as strong as naturally possible, then I urge you to take advantage of this most powerful information TODAY.

I've walked in your shoes, searching and researching weight training theory, bodybuilding supplements and training table protocols since 1985 in pursuit of maximum muscle, strength and winning sports performance.

LEARN from my hundreds of hours of gym and lab trials. Possess the knowledge of countless real life athlete studies that power the FACTS revealed inside the pages of The Blueprint for Big Muscle Building.

The Blueprint 4.0 for Big Muscle Building lets you in on

- The secret to MAXIMIZING muscle building, for life, in five fast days.
- Why brief muscle tissue breakdown is fundamental to your success, along with the surprising what/when/where and how keys to doing it exactly right.
- The strategic way to turn an overtrained/catabolic state into a

THE BLUEPRINT FOR BIG MUSCLE BUILDING

month+ of SUPERCHARGED size and strength gains. It's eye-opening information.
- The truth about how the Soviet sports machine created "supermen" with organic bodybuilding supplements. Hint: It's the opposite of what you've heard.
- The go-to strategy that will FORCE your body to pack on muscle mass.
- How to manipulate ATP dependency (in a way even steroids can't do) and free yourself to realize your true potential to become stronger–much stronger!
- The ONE natural bodybuilding supplement that doubles muscle building. The secret is not just knowing what it is, but WHEN to use it. I reveal the name, discount source and precisely how to use it to double your muscle building.
- The 4 distinct physiological states you must create and how to stagger them to maximize your training, nutrition and bodybuilding supplements. You've seen it; progress comes and goes in spurts and seems totally "hit or miss". With your "BLUEPRINT" in hand, you'll be expertly planning each phase for stunning gains!
- The lowdown on breaking through ANY plateau that holds you back.
- Why some get results from bodybuilding supplements, and others don't. Truth is, it's dependent on the state your body is in when you use supplements and IF it's a legit product. Learn how to get the most bang for the buck from the supplements that really work. I also flat-out EXPOSE the junk ones that don't work at all.
- How to build muscle mass and get stronger from EVERY single workout by knowing how to eat at mealtime to maximize growth and recovery.
- You'll know exactly what to eat, when to eat, and even how to "pig out" for gains!

The "BLUEPRINT" will forever change your physique. It will smarten you up to the real bodybuilding supplements worth your time and money. It will change how your training partners and others view you–and most importantly, it will change YOU.

Once you put your Biologically Perfect BLUEPRINT into action there will be no stopping you. Your smart investment in yourself will pay a lifetime of dividends. This is the intelligent way to add permanent, real muscle mass to your frame and get stronger than you've ever imagined.

So, what will it be?

Are you ready to arm yourself with the power to grow major league muscle?

The Blueprint Meteoric

The Final Frontier, For The Drug-Free Athlete!

The infamous steroid guru's figured this out and increasingly touted an array of anabolic drugs to force one's physiology into a state of rapid muscle building.

So, is there a natural way to "steroid-like gains" in muscle mass and super strength without the bad risk-to-benefit ratio of bodybuilding drugs?

The BP Meteoric then, seeks to deliver it ALL—and FAST!
What does this mean? It means you'll get big, shredded and in record time.

You'll find ALL of the following, by investing in the Blueprint Meteoric:

- A fantastic level of Conditioning/General Physical Preparedness (GPP).
- You'll build a solid base at the bottom your fitness pyramid, which brings us to…
- Incredible Alpha/Absolute Strength that Blueprint 2.0 was famous for, which is the foundation EVERY other type of strength is built upon.
- Massive increase in Beta Strength/Total Tonnage done per unit of time. This is the physiological trigger for muscle growth, and its "juiced" considerably when Alpha Strength is boosted prior. Blueprint 3.0 introduced this trick via coupling several different training modalities. We accomplish something better here—FASTER THAN ANY OTHER PROGRAM OUT THERE.
- How to increase growth hormone naturally, even more so than injectable growth-hormone.
- The ability to repeat these hyper-gains for MONTHS on end—not weeks!

The BP Meteoric is a repeating 8-week cycle that draws upon three different energy systems.

This doesn't come without sacrifice.

Much of what's called for here requires strict adherence to the new training and dietary measures we've created in order to pull this off. That's consistent with what made Blueprint 3.0 so successful, and it's important to make the distinction.

The BP Meteoric isn't for everyone, but for those that like being told exactly what to do, when and why—they'll thrive on it.

It will likely be the last training system needed, for those of us who desire to carry forward our version of perfection, into an imperfect world.

Finally, the fundamental change inherent in The Blueprint Meteoric is the speed, at which the "unorthodox" unfolds.

It would seem the body's adaptive response can be further amplified, given the careful arrangement of certain exercise, diet and supplementation fundamentals. It became clear for example, that what distinguished The Blueprint 2.0 and 3.0 from any other training system was that the speed of methodical change was faster. Faster than any other program out there.

Gratefully and not by coincidence, so were the results. In fact, the biggest barrier to entry for those curious about Blueprint quickly became, "This is too good to be true." Yet it is true, and there are people all over the world today that are the living, breathing truth.

You want it all? Now you have it...

Prepare to take the governors off your muscle growth...

This training system is the marriage of 3 very different workouts over the course of a week, dovetailing with a new diet we've paired it with. If you know our other literary works, you know this: We don't rehash hash.

What you're about to read will challenge everything you know, yet vault you to a level of size, strength and conditioning that leaves your friends and family dumbfounded. Too good to be true? That's what they said about The Blueprint 2.0 and 3.0.

SPECIAL REPORT

Building The Perfect Anabolic Agent: Progenadren

The Progenadren Report will explain how to make an orally active anabolic agent, working through both hormonal/non-hormonal pathways.

Two servings/day will absolutely, positively pack on noticeable lean body mass as validated in the gym, in the mirror, on the tape measure and on the scale.

We have no hesitation in saying it's every bit as effective as many illegal AAS, and all ingredients are readily available both in the U.S. and in Europe.

SPECIAL REPORT

Laxogenin: Where To Find The Genuine Article, And How to Stack it

The Laxogenin Report will explain how to make the ultimate non-hormonal anabolic agent, for use by drug-tested/competitive athletes or those not willing to use PH or AAS due to shutdown/legal issues, etc.

SPECIAL REPORT

STILL LEGAL BUT NOT FOR LONG: ULTIMATE RELAXATION AND CHILL PILLS—A HOW TO GUIDE

The Ultimate Relaxation and Chill Pill Report will detail what is, in our opinion, the strongest relaxation/chill supplements you can use—ANYWHERE. These supplements are so powerful, we're surprised they're still legal. Big statement, but once you try these you'll likely agree.

Within the realm sports nutrition, not many supplements produce a "feelable" effect. Not so with these babies, and there will be no "I think it's working…" situation here.

SPECIAL REPORT

How to Combine 3 Over-the-Shelf Nutraceuticals That Fry-Off Body Fat

Collectively, the ingredients in this Special Report will fry off body fat by increasing thermogenesis, suppressing appetite and recycling the process—keeping it going longer and stronger.

The best part? The entire stack will run you a whopping $9.98 when purchased online, and last you seemingly forever.

Hands down the most effective over-the-shelf fat loss stack, at pennies on the dollar…

SPECIAL REPORT

RICOCHET RABBIT FAT LOSS: QUICKER THAN A HICCUP, BURNS FAT LIKE BUTTER IN A MICROWAVE

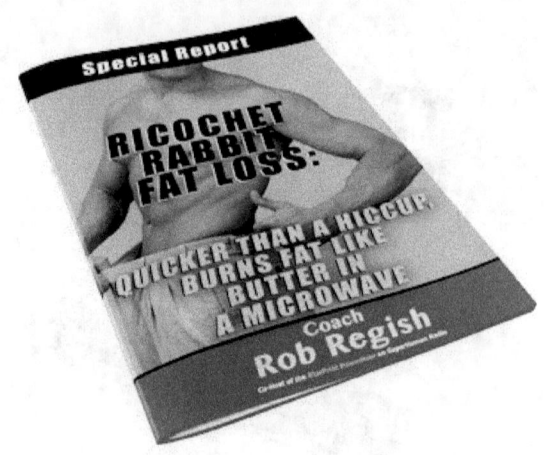

Collectively, the ingredients in this Special Report will fry off body fat by increasing thermogenesis, suppressing appetite and recycling the process—keeping it going longer and stronger.

There are supplements that give you energy, others that burn fat and some that preserve lean body mass. There are even supplements that boost testosterone levels. But there is NOTHING that does ALL of these things. Until now…

SPECIAL REPORT

Neurobolt: Building the Most Potent Nootropic for Performance Enhancement

The Neurobolt Report will explain how to make a nootropic that lights up your central nervous system like a Christmas tree, allowing you to lift heavier. It doesn't rattle you like ephedrine, but there's no crash either. There's been an explosion of products in the pre-workout/energy category over the years and not without reason: Consumers can FEEL them. It's rare for any nutritional supplement to produce results, but thermogenics sure fall into this category. Still, they have their downsides. Chief among these are over-stimulating the user and using excessive amounts of caffeine (one-dimensional). Yet, there IS another category that reliably enhances performance—nootropics.

Loosely stated, nootropics are also referred to as smart drugs, memory enhancers, neuro-enhancer, cognitive enhancers, and intelligence enhancers. They can take the form of drugs, supplements, functional foods and hybrids that improve mental function. That improvement in mental function is measured by assessing things such as memory, motivation and sustained performance while on task.

SPECIAL REPORT

Protein Synthesis

A supplement that doubles muscle-growth, triples fat loss and delivers a 7-hour increase in protein synthesis for under $10/month!

SPECIAL REPORT

The Blueprint Mass Stack

In the process of crafting The Blueprint 4.0, new training techniques were introduced that placed a severe stress on the trainee. It was time to update The Blueprint Mass Stack.

I teamed up with the MASS research and development to look at alternatives. If you're looking to take your training to the next level, I can't recommend the new Blueprint Mass Stack highly enough.

THE "DRINK"

Build Muscle, Lose Fat... FAST!

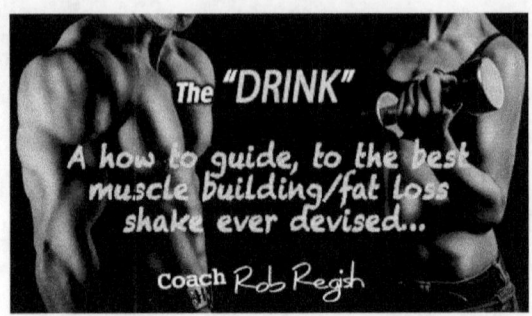

A VIDEO how-to guide to the best muscle building/fat loss shake ever devised...

Why You Need This Drink:

- It's the most powerful "Weight Gainer" you'll ever experience
- Amazing Fat Loss properties
- Improve Protein Digestion, Uptake and Utilization
- Quick Results!
- and Much More!

THE HORMONE OPTIMIZATION COURSE

All About Hormones!

Jam-Packed with Information About How to Optimize your Hormone Levels, Including Testosterone, Growth Hormones & Cortisol.

You really don't want to miss this information!

Here's a fraction of what you'll learn in this video presentation:

- Optimizing Testosterone Levels
- Adaptogen
- NDHEA
- Quick Results!
- And Much More!

SUPPLEMENTS FORMULATED BY COACH ROB REGISH

PROGENADREX

Accelerate Muscle Growth, Nothing Less!

Progenadrex's sole reason for being is to accelerate muscle growth, nothing less. This isn't an easy thing to do, especially given the fact that governments have taken away most hormones. In the absence of being able to give you supraphysiological test and growth hormone levels, it leverages the most powerful anabolic you can put into your body: Food.

The ingredients have been carefully selected to maximize every morsel of food that you eat, be it protein carbs or fats. It absolutely excels at stuffing the muscle full of glycogen, hygroscopic amino acids and, of course, water and other energy compounds. Most importantly, it accelerates lean body mass gains secondary to growth being stimulated via overload.

Anacyclus Pyrethrum Ethanol Extract (5:1)

In 2010 researchers at the Hari Singh Gour University in India published the results of an animal study showing Anacyclus stimulated the sexual behavior of rats in a way that resembled the effect of testosterone[6]. The researchers had already established how Anacyclus boosts the synthesis of testosterone. Specifically, doubling it. We'll see why that's important later, but for now know that it provides an androgen boost so coveted by athletes. More importantly this ingredient is the king of substrate storage, swelling the muscle cell with glycogen.

By all accounts, you'll crave more carbs and realize much greater muscle fulness.

Remember, the suffix is hydrate. For every gram of glycogen stored, your body pulls in nearly three grams of water with it, effectively tripling muscle cell volume. Two other important points: The amount of AP in Progenadrex is proprietary, but falls well within the effective anabolic ranges established in the literature. You'll note one other important point: ONLY the ethanol extract has been tested and found to double testosterone. "Supplementation of anacyclus pyrethrum ethanolic root extract (50–150 mg/kg) over 28 days in rats noted dose-dependent increases in testosterone and luteinizing hormone to approximately two-fold of the baseline[7]."

Laxogenin

Lax is an ingredient I know well, perhaps better than anyone in the industry given my 20-year history with it. It's no stretch to say I've used every Lax product going back to the original Mesobolin, put out by Amino Discounters in the early 1990s. Yet, companies have been missing a key qualifier for Laxogenin to exert its full effects: An optimal androgen level. For example, one of Syrov's papers details Laxogenin and how it works. From "An Experimental Study On The Anabolic Activities of 6-Keto Derivatives Of Some Natural Sapogenins", and I quote "Castratration of the rats resulted in 26%

6   http://www.ncbi.nlm.nih.gov/pubmed/20727332
7   http://examine.com/supplements/Anacyclus+pyrethrum/#ref1

less growth vs. intact rats of the same age." In the even rarer companion paper I have, "Novel, Natural and Non-Hormonal Anabolic Agents Derived From Plants," this point is again hammered home, "Castration of the animals weakens the anabolic effects of Laxogenin." This tells us that some level of testosterone/androgen must be present to exert its full effects.

Acting as testosterone mimetic or catalyst, Anacylus P. ensures Laxogenin's full potential is realized by doubling your test. So we've boosted testosterone, glycogen storage and maximized protein synthesis with just two ingredients. Can it get any better than this? Yes, it can. Enter Creatine HCL, R-ALA and disodium phosphate.

Creatine HCL

It's generally agreed that creatine hydrochloride is many times more soluble in water than creatine monohydrate. Due to its higher solubility, the recommended dosage for creatine hydrochloride is much lower than that for monohydrate. De facto, there is no loading dose necessary, nor mixing up grams of gritty powders or bloat.

Despite this, Progenadrex contains a higher than usual amount of Creatine HCL given the broader formula's ability to stuff muscles full of glucose, H2O, hygroscopic amino acids and other goodies. As we'll soon see, both R-ALA and Di Sodium Phosphate ramp up creatine uptake as well.

R-ALA/Biotin

It's unquestionably the R isomer of alpha-lipoic acid that enhances the effect of creatine. The effect of the L isomer is less, according to research[8]. This is especially true if you're co-ingesting with carbohydrates like you should, as Progenadrex was designed to amplify the most powerful anabolic you can put into your body: Food.

---

8 http://www.ncbi.nlm.nih.gov/pubmed/9252495

R-ALA/Laxogenin Synergy

Previously, I've expounded the virtues of Laxogenin's anti-inflammatory effects. The former owner of Beyond-A-Century (who at the time sold "Anabolica", an exceptional Lax product) told me he sold, "caseloads" to lupus patients, and other persons afflicted with pro-inflammatory conditions.

Little known fact: When you REALLY scrub the research on R-ALA, it isn't the glucose disposal/antioxidant or other benefits that stand out. It's the anti-inflammatory effects in HUMAN studies, that really grab your attention.
"In humans, a clinical trial noted a 15% serum reduction in levels of interleukin-6 (an inflammatory marker) following 4 weeks of 300 mg racemic ALA supplementation. [120]". Thus, the Laxogenin/R-ALA tag team works through multiple pathways to increase protein synthesis, improve creatine uptake and squelch inflammation leading to incredibly fast recovery from exercise.

Biotin is added to prevent the depletion of such, when high dose ALA is used. Without it, you're going to be running into skin issues your first week. Every base has been covered, with nothing left to chance.

Finally, we get to

Sodium Phosphate

It's often overlooked, but sodium is even more important for creatine uptake than insulin according to studies done in several peer reviewed medical journals*. By providing a precise dose along with creatine hcl and r-ala, you're guaranteed to maximize creatine uptake, utilization and performance where other products fail.

BOTTOM LINE:

It's faster, it works better and your results come quicker.

Now you can grow as fast with Progenadrex, as you can recover with Synthagen. With Progenadrex, you'll rapidly achieve greater muscle size, strength and pumps like you're on a PH. Best of all, there's no PCT therapy needed, as the ingredients have been documented quite safe and in fact, healthy.

MASS PRO SYNTHAGEN

IF YOU'RE NOT GROWING, IT'S LIKELY YOU'RE NOT RECOVERING FROM YOUR WORKOUTS EITHER.

Since recovery always precedes growth, **Synthagen** is what's needed to unlock your growth potential.

Discover the POWER of ProtoGeneX™ for yourself. A proprietary, 10 Amino Acid Matrix:

- **L-Leucine**
- **L-Lysine**
- **L-Phenylalanine**
- **L-Valine**
- **L-Threonine**

- L-Isoleucine
- L-Methionine
- L-Histidine
- L-Taurine
- L-Tryptophan

Omni-Potent Nutrition Optimization

It's important to point out the three Branched Chain Amino Acids stimulate protein synthesis. Essential Amino Acids have all nine, allowing you to complete the process of growing new muscle.

Big difference!

It took two years, 17 prototypes and many untold hours to arrive at the EAA ratios used in Synthagen. We encourage you to put to the test!

MASS PRO SYNTHAGEN SUBSTRATES

Synthagen doesn't stop there, not by a longshot. Protein synthesis is further magnified and its duration extended via including one of a kind Rhaponticum Carthamoides Extract. This very special, rare species has been shown to increase both the speed and activity in the ribosome (or factory), with which these amino acids are assembled. In simple terms, you build muscle faster.

It also does things no other supplement can: It recycles nucleotide pools, boost ATP three different ways (creatine only works via one), vastly improves levels of intracellular buffering agents, allowing you to train harder and longer. The simultaneous increase of carnosine AND beta-alanine accelerates wound healing, and the whole process is recycled and extended for up to six hours, by supplying additional methyl donors in the liver.

MASS PRO Synthagen delivers strong protein synthesis signaling while providing the "building blocks" and elite substrates that grow new muscle—precisely when and where your body needs them most.

Protein synthesis must include the essential amino acids. For, if even a single EAA is missing, no muscle can be built or repaired—hence the term, "essential." MASS PRO Synthagen™ formula provides ALL of the essential amino acids in proven potencies and in circulation concurrently with very powerful substrates to optimally leverage omnipotent effects, in particular vastly accelerated protein synthesis.

Branched Chain Amino Acids (BCAA) also spike protein synthesis, so for maximum results a strong shot of the "tested positive" proprietary BCAA's as found in MASS PRO Amino are included. The BCAA's are key signaling agents, and the full ProtoGeneX (proto-gene-ten) Amino Acid Matrix literally floods your cells with every single amino acid proven to build, repair and replenish muscle tissue.

MASS PRO Synthagen closes the gap between safe, smart supplementation and harmful performance drugs like never before. It works so well some may question, but be assured this elite natural formula is 100% drug/hormone-free and equally effective for both sexes without restriction.

MASS PRO Synthagen draws upon 20 years of Muscle And Sports Science® innovations, combined with the cutting-edge research and weight room winning insights of Coach Rob Regish (Author of "The Blueprint for BIG Muscle Building" and weekly Super Human Radio Contributor).

MASS PRO Synthagen advances nutrition optimization and sports enhancements to a virtually fail-proof region, because it "auto-corrects" so many common pitfalls that can occur with anyone's training, diet and supplementation—even top professional athletes.

The latest MASS PRO addition, called SYNTHAGEN, facilitates extremely fast muscle recovery from high intensity exercise—while near instantly replenishing burned cellular energy stores. It's unlike anything you've seen before.

THINK about it—These two positive effects are GLOBAL in scope. The benefits from Synthagen are, in fact, SO VERY PRONOUNCED that many first-time users react with stunned silence—or, they start telling everyone they know and care about to buy up a year's supply!

Seeing is believing, but MASS PRO SYNTHAGEN ("MPS" for short) is being widely heralded as the most effective drug-free recovery agent to ever hit the health and fitness marketplace.

This formulation sports professional, tangible dosages of no-less than 16 nutraceuticals, all working in concert to optimize muscle while simultaneously restoring raw cellular energy.

Synthagen contains the advanced ProtoGeneX Amino Acid Matrix, a marvel all on its own, to very rapidly stimulate and sustain an elevated state of protein synthesis. It fuels, it feeds, and it's long lasting.

To be very clear-MASS PRO SYNTHAGEN accomplishes its goals without any stimulants or hormones, and it can be used safely and effectively by men and women, the young—and the not so young!

Why is Synthagen so unique?

It effectively "green lights" every bodily function conducive to growing muscle, recovering from exercise and keeping one's metabolism burning fat and performing at its physical peak.

Consider the following illustration:

Imagine yourself as being in a race, at the start of a 10-mile long closed course right through town. At the finish line is the winners trophy representing top muscle/lowest body fat/highest performance.

At each mile marker is an intersection that represents potential rate limiting qualifiers to the finish line. For example, if even ONE essential amino acid is not in place when needed (and most protein supplements ARE missing one, two, or three ESSENTIALS aminos!), well, that's a big old fat rate limiting RED STOP LIGHT.

Your progress comes to a screeching HALT as the body searches for the vital, missing amino acid. Hit just a few rate limiting red lights and you'll be lucky to stumble in to finish the race, never mind winning FIRST PLACE.

Here's THE UPSIDE—Imagine what having all green lights can do for you … because SYNTHAGEN effectively turns every single rate limiting red light, GREEN!

Personal achievement soars with Synthagen by eliminating GLOBAL rate limitations. Smart coaches are also discovering this is the advantage to turn an also-ran team, into a team of run away CHAMPIONS.

FACT: No other sports supplement is targeted to identify and eliminate the roadblocks to ELITE level success on this scale, with absolute precision. Nothing. This is the genesis of MASS PRO SYNTHAGEN.

110% unique, original, and EXCLUSIVE.

CAUTION:

Synthagen allows you to recover so quickly from training that we must SERIOUSLY warn users to be careful not to overtrain. A few rest days weekly are needed and advised, even if you do feel you can train every single day, EVEN MULTIPLE SESSIONS with Synthagen on your side.

MANY report an energized enlightenment of sorts following their first Synthagen doses, but it's difficult to describe since it is a very "clean" (non-stimulant), naturally occurring benefit of nutrition optimization.

MASS PRO SYNTHAGEN appears to be a natural nootropic due to its elevation of blood flow to BOTH the body AND the BRAIN, for up to six hours.

This elevation was engineered in from the onset to ensure Synthagen's ingredients and any foods you eat with it get to your muscle tissue FAST and efficiently. The nootropic/feel great effects were an unanticipated bonus which became apparent during R&D testing and illustrates just how many bodily systems stand to benefit.

One other thing to note is that multiple ingredients in Synthagen "back up," team and string together with each other like a safety net to ensure "fail-proof" success for all, regardless of age or gender.

This said, we can't help but be proud of the "I feel like my old self again!" Synthagen reviews flooding in from outspoken advocates in life extension and life enhancement circles.

Is there a way to boost Testosterone and growth hormone with Synthagen to max out muscle and cuts, together?

Synthagen is an advanced "all-arounder" supplement you can employ strategically in and around workouts, and/or at various other targeted times of the day or night. All on its own, or together with other proven items.

Synthagen can both replace multiple marginal supplements you've been using, and also significantly enhance uptake and utilization of ANY time proven formulas/foods you currently enjoy success with.

The top complimentary nutraceuticals people are reporting as the best to stack with Synthagen are:

- A legitimate testosterone booster like "Adaptogen N," especially for men over the age of 30.
- 'MASS PRO Ultimate Whey Protein, to ensure varied world class dietary protein is consumed Tart Cherry Juice Extract, which is generating a LOT of positive anti-aging Synthagen reviews.
- 'Burn It Up' caps, taken before endurance sports and for those times you need abundant 'brain fuel.'
- TranQuilogen, a now-popular 'stack' with Synthagen for anti-inflammation and natural pain relief.

- 'Gamma GH' is very popular for a boost in growth hormone, tendon strength and a GREAT night's restorative sleep.
- 'BluePrint for Big Muscle Building' devotees typically stack 'MASS PRO SYNTHAGEN' with 'KA' (Kre-Anabolyn ActivECDY).

MASS PRO SYNTHAGEN™ is in very high demand, and available on a first come, first served basis.

Every batch to date has sold out in record time. Avoid delay, lock in your personal supplies.

Order NOW to have MASS PRO Synthagen delivered FAST to your door.

MASS PRO Synthagen™ is an Exclusive, Proprietary Formula and 'Nutrition Optimization' is a Service Mark of MUSCLE MASS INC.

TRANQUILOGEN

IF YOU'RE DRAGGING YOURSELF TO THE GYM AND FEELING BEAT UP, OR HAVE NIGGLING LITTLE INJURIES THAT JUST WON'T GO AWAY, YOU NEED TRANQUILOGEN.

TranQuilogen's unique formula sparks mental and physical rejuvenation, complete with pain relief.

It's like turning back the clock, and has finally allowed many trainees to gain again whereas before injuries were holding them back. It accomplishes this by positively modulating both body and brain chemistry with research proven levels of healthy, Validated Full Spectrum nutraceuticals.

If you work a high stress job, you really need this stuff!

Proven Ingredients:

Rhodiola Rosea VFS Extract

You get top-shelf Verified Full Spectrum Rhodiola Rosea, standardized for the active ingredients straight out of Russia—where the most potent stuff grows. It revitalizes mind and body, rebalancing epi/nor-epinephrine and cortisol levels thrown out of whack, given our stress riddled lives.

CurcuClear Curcumin

Ditto for the CurcuClear Curcumin concentrate we use. The anti-inflammatory/cancer-fighting benefits aside, this is one potent pain killer—working to actually heal injuries, not just cover them up. It's been called, "The Herbal Clenbuterol" by no less an authority than ErgoLog.com.

5-HTP, Picamilon

Another nootropic from Russia and high dose Astaxanthin round out the formula, delivering what may be the most potent 1 cap/feel good dose product of its kind. 2 caps/day during stressful times makes a world of difference, and you'll feel it both in your mind and body.

Plus…

The highest potency **Natural Source Astaxanthin** and **Patented Bioperine**. All, at or above research trial proven potency levels, in convenient **Chlorophyllin** enhanced capsules.

No Fluff. No Fillers.
REAL RESULTS YOU CAN FEEL.

TranQuilogen™ is a professional, proprietary formula which works to promote maximum mental and physical relaxation, restoration and rejuvenation.

MEET COACH ROB REGISH

For almost 30 years, Coach Rob has devoted his life to the pursuit of mastering physical culture. He is a former power-lifter, accomplished author, radio personality, product-formulator and sought-after consultant, covering a broad range of topics in the field.

Why Coach Rob can help you get on the road to Gainsville—in the FAST lane:

- **Author of the Blueprint Series Books**
  - *The Blueprint for Big Muscle Building* (2.0, 3.0 & 4.0)
  - *The Blueprint Meteoric.*
- **Weekly contributor to popular radio shows,** such as **The Blue Print Power Hour** on Super Human Radio and Fiorillo Barbell's **Motivation & Muscle** Podcast. He also has his own podcast, **MuscleU.**
- **Author of "The Blueprint Bulletin,"** a sought-after monthly newsletter filled with the absolute latest and greatest information!
- **Product Formulator.** Products issued from the cutting-edge research and weight-room winning insights. These quality dietary supplements are designed to accelerate muscle growth, fat loss and promote anti-aging and longevity.

- Mass Pro Synthagen
- TranQuilogen
- Progenadrex

Rob lives his training every day, just like you. In his mid-forties, he can still be found doing one arm pushups and training hard in the gym. And just like you he takes this lifestyle seriously, with an eye for RESULTS. After all, RESULTS are what really matter. So learn from his hard-won knowledge and wisdom.

<u>CoachRobRegish.com</u>

NEXT STEPS

Thanks again for reading this book. If you haven't received your gifts yet, please take a second to register your book.

You'll automatically receive the following items to support your journey:

```
┌ ─ ─ ─ ─ ─ ─ ─ ─ ─ ┐
│    The Blueprint Bulletin,    │
│  Fast Fat Loss - Special Report,  │
│   "The Drink" - Learn How to Make   │
│      The Best Muscle Building/      │
│        Fat Loss Shake Ever!         │
│      Video Training program.        │
└ ─ ─ ─ ─ ─ ─ ─ ─ ─ ┘
```

Simply visit:

FastMuscleBook.com

www.ingramcontent.com/pod-product-compliance
Lightning Source LLC
LaVergne TN
LVHW051601070426
835507LV00021B/2704